Appellate Court Delay

Structural Responses to the Problems of Volume and Delay

John A. Martin
Elizabeth A. Prescott

Edited and with a Foreword by
Michael J. Hudson

A Publication of the
National Center for State Courts
Williamsburg, Virginia

Copyright © 1981 by The National Center for State Courts
Printed in the United States of America

Library of Congress Cataloging in Publication Data
Martin, John A.
   Appellate court delay.

   Includes bibliographical references.
   1. Court congestion and delay—United States—
States. 2. Appellate courts—United States—
States. I. Prescott, Elizabeth A. II. Hudson,
Michael J.   III. National Center for State Courts.
IV. Title.

KF8727.M37	347.73′8	81-11044
ISBN 0-89656-048-1	347.3078	AACR2

This research was conducted under Grants No. 78-DF-AX-0021 and No. 79-DF-AX-0082, awarded to the National Center for State Courts by the Law Enforcement Assistance Administration of the U.S. Department of Justice. Additional funding was supplied by the Charles E. Culpeper Foundation. Points of view or opinions stated in this document are those of the authors and do not necessarily represent the official position or policies of the U.S. Department of Justice, the Charles E. Culpeper Foundation, the National Center for State Courts, or the project advisory board. The Law Enforcement Assistance Administration reserves the right to reproduce, publish, translate, or otherwise use, and to authorize others to publish and use, any or all parts of the copyright material contained in this publication.

Table of Contents

Foreword v

Preface viii

Executive Summary xii

Chapter 1. An Introduction to This Study 1
   Questions Investigated 2
   Information Sources 3
   The Ten Sample Courts 3

Chapter 2. Appellate Delay and Court Reform 6
   A Conceptual Framework for Classifying Solutions 7
   A Brief Critique of Proposed Solutions 9
      Type I Solutions 9
      Type II Solutions 11
      Type III Solutions 14
      Type IV Solutions 15

Chapter 3. Measuring Processing Time and Delay 17
   Total Case Processing Time 18
   Components of Total Case Processing Time 19
   The Predecision Phase 22
   The Decision-Making Phase 29
   General Patterns Among Courts 32

Chapter 4. Caseload and Delay 36
   Questions Investigated 36
   Principal Findings 37
      Volume and Delay 37
      Case Types and Delay 42
      Processing Variables and Delay 45

Chapter 5, Structure, Organization, and Procedure as Correlates of Case Processing Time: the Predecision Phase 50
   Assessing the Impact of Organization and Procedure 50
   Total Processing Time 51
      Step 1 Time 53
      Extension Policies 53
      Step 2 Time 61
      Argument-Scheduling Practices 61
      Assignment Procedures 66

Chapter 6. Case Processing Time During the Decision Phase 68
   Organization of Decision-Making Authority 68
      Panel Structure 69
      Panel Conflicts 69
      Analysis 70
      Summary Disposition 71
   Decisions and Opinions 71
      Opinion Content 72
      Judges' Perceptions of Their Role in the
        Appellate Process 73

Chapter 7. An Incremental Appellate Reform Strategy 77
   Philosophy and Method 77
   Elements of an Incremental Court Reform Strategy 78
   Assessing the Appellate System and Identifying
      Specific Problems 79
   Selecting and Implementing Techniques for
      Court Improvement 81
   Evaluating Techniques 82

Appendix A: Time Interval Distributions 84

Appendix B: Delay Statistics 100

**Appendix C: Correlation of Volume with Delay:
              Summary** 118

Appendix D: Case-Characteristics Breakdowns 126

Appendix E: Uniform Data-Collection Instrument 138

Afterwords
   Anne N. Costain: Reducing Delay in Government
      Institutions 146
   Robert A. Leflar: Delay in Appellate Courts 151
   Alfred Blumstein: Court Delay and Queueing Theory 155

Foreword

This volume represents three years of empirical research and analysis in appellate courts. Throughout this effort, our primary goal has been to increase our knowledge of the appellate process, and by doing so to make it possible to design better methods for reducing delay and contending with rising volume in appellate systems.

At the same time, we recognize that these findings may have implications beyond those we have discussed specifically in the text, and that as custodians of the public's money, we have an obligation to make the findings as accessible as possible to audiences representing a variety of disciplines.

Accordingly, authorities who are themselves well qualified to address a variety of audiences reviewed the manuscript and provided suggestions and criticisms, and in addition wrote the commentaries on the findings and their implications. These commentaries are presented at the end of this volume.

Professor Anne N. Costain, of the University of Colorado, comments thoughtfully on how this research into the judicial system may suggest methods of improving the other two branches of government. Speaking as a political scientist, she measures these methods against standards of quality developed within her discipline and discusses the questions that then arise.

Professor Robert A. Leflar, of the University of Arkansas Law School, is well known as a major force for appellate court reform in many forums, including the Arkansas Supreme Court, the American Bar Association's Committee on Standards of Judicial Conduct, and the Appellate Judges' Seminar of the New York University School of Law. His commentary reviews the major findings of this study in the light of his experience and his study of the field. His observations will be of interest to anyone involved in improving appellate justice.

Professor Alfred Blumstein, of Carnegie-Mellon University, a leader in the field of operations research, discusses in his commentary the ways in which "queueing theory" may illuminate the findings of this research and perhaps even help to form the framework for future study into the quality of appellate justice, building upon the quantitative research presented in this volume. We hope that Professor Blumstein's precise observations will help make this research more pertinent to planners, educators, and public administrators.

I encourage the reader to study these comments carefully. They are valuable both in themselves and as vehicles for expanding the possible uses of this research.

Since the inception of the National Center for State Courts, appellate courts have been a prime focus of Center studies. Early work assessed practices, particularly the use of central staff, in Illinois, New

Jersey, Nebraska, and Virginia. Regional office analytic work in this early period was undertaken in the California Court of Appeals, the 4th District Court of Appeals of Florida, and the Delaware Supreme Court. Coincidentally, specialized studies were completed: for example, judicial opinion-publishing practices in the Northeast, continuing judicial education for Alabama appellate judges, and a nonjudicial personnel study in the Massachusetts Supreme Judicial Court and Appeals Court. Other studies have been conducted in Washington, Wisconsin, Rhode Island, Pennsylvania, Utah, and Connecticut.

A major report examining traditional functions of appeals and efficiency-promoting alternatives was published by the Center as *Justice on Appeal,* by Carrington, Meador, and Rosenberg. In 1975, the National Center cosponsored, with the Federal Judicial Center, a National Conference on Appellate Justice, in San Diego. Appellate court studies in such diverse areas as recordkeeping, automated processing, unpublished opinions, clerks' office management, and law libraries have been prepared for Alaska, Minnesota, California, Idaho, New Jersey, and West Virginia. National Center studies in court reporting services in several states have also proven valuable in improving appellate courts' performance.

Major research undertaken as part of Phase I of the Appellate Justice Improvement Project included the preparation of three works, *Volume and Delay in Appellate Courts: Some Preliminary Findings from a National Survey, Volume and Delay in State Appellate Courts: Problems and Responses* and *Bibliography: State Appellate Court Workload and Delay.* The second phase of the project resulted in several reports, scientific evaluation of demonstration projects, technical assistance in the form of reports, site visits and correspondence, a series of regional appellate court workshops, and the preparation of this volume.

This book is, then, but one facet of the many activities of the Appellate Justice Improvement Project, described in the authors' Preface, and the project is in turn the latest in a continuum of work by the National Center for State Courts directed at improving appellate justice. In their Preface the authors acknowledge the substantial contributions of many people to this book and to its findings. I concur and add my appreciation to theirs. In addition, I wish to acknowledge here the contributions of certain people whose dedication and skill helped make it possible for the project to succeed and to deliver its many products of which this book is one.

One of the members of the project's staff has been Cynthia Easterling, who has contributed immensely and with exceptional diplomacy to the successful coordination of this project.

The effectiveness of the project is in many ways due to the enthusiasm and dedication of the director of the Northeastern Regional Office, Samuel Conti. The project has benefited especially from his adherence to the very highest standards in the preparation of studies and publications.

It is his express aim that publications of his office shall whenever possible advance the state of the art, and it is our hope that the work and publications of this project have met that standard.

Nicholas Demos, the LEAA Project Monitor, has been scrupulous in his insistence that the public receive full value for its money; and the productivity of the Project is due in no small part to him.

JANUARY 1981   MICHAEL J. HUDSON
Project Director
Appellate Justice Improvement Project

Preface

This book represents the findings of an examination of volume and delay in several state appellate courts. It focuses on appellate court operations in ten courts located in ten states nationwide. The courts included in the study were not chosen as representative of the "best" or "worst" appellate courts in the country. Our intention, rather, was to examine a broad mix of appellate courts from various parts of the country, including courts with dissimilar case volumes, operating within differing organizational structures and following a variety of procedures.

The four goals of this volume are, first, to provide an overview of the environments in which these appellate courts operate and to describe the case processing time in each unique environment; second, to determine how appellate delay can be defined and reliably measured; third, to identify as many correlates of appellate case processing time as possible and to isolate and determine the importance of each such correlate as a potential source of delay; and finally, to formulate conclusions concerning the effectiveness of reforms designed to combat appellate court delay. To the extent that these four goals have been met, an informative source document will have been provided from which judges, court personnel, attorneys, litigants, scholars, and the general public may assess the doing of justice in the appellate court forum.

Publication of this volume represents but one product of a multi-faceted study undertaken by the National Center for State Courts: the Appellate Justice Improvement Project. Other publications prepared by this project's staff include an extensive review of previous literature on appellate court delay;[1] a bibliography of 300 studies of the appellate process;[2] and a series of monographs examining the problems of delay in specific appellate jurisdictions.[3]

---

1. S. L. Wasby, T. B. Marvell, and A. B. Aikman, *Volume and Delay in State Appellate Courts: Problems and Responses* (Williamsburg, Va.: National Center for State Courts, 1979).

2. T. B. Marvell, *Bibliography: State Appellate Caseload and Delay* (Williamsburg, Va.: National Center for State Courts, 1979).

3. The following courts are examined in individual reports: the Colorado Court of Appeals; the Florida Supreme Court; the Florida First District Court of Appeal; the Illinois Appellate Court, First District; the Indiana Court of Appeals; the Montana Supreme Court; the Nebraska Supreme Court; the New Jersey Superior Court, Appellate Division; the Ohio Court of Appeals, Eighth District; the Oregon Court of Appeals; and the Virginia Supreme Court. These reports are available as the Volume and Delay Staff Study Series, by J. A. Martin and E. A. Prescott (North Andover, Mass.: National Center for State Courts, 1980). Series editor Michael J. Hudson, Project Director.

Technical assistance, experimentation, and rigorous evaluation have also been fundamental components of the project. The project established experimental demonstration programs to test proposed solutions to the problems of delay and volume in four diverse appellate jurisdictions.[4] Technical assistance has encompassed a variety of tasks, such as responding to requests for information and advice submitted by appellate court personnel throughout the country, undertaking site visits to analyze particular court problems and develop appropriate remedies, and conducting regional problem-solving workshops and seminars.

As often happens in a project with numerous, diverse goals, many organizations and individuals have made substantial contributions. We would like to acknowledge their contributions and express our gratitude.

The enduring financial support of the Law Enforcement Assistance Administration of the U.S. Department of Justice and the Charles E. Culpeper Foundation are gratefully acknowledged. Foremost on the list of individuals to thank are past and present members of the project advisory board, who provided periodic review of materials and invaluable assistance: Hon. John V. Corrigan, Ohio Court of Appeals, Eighth District; Mr. Ron L. Dzierbicki, Michigan Court of Appeals; Hon. Jerome Farris, United States Court of Appeals, Ninth Circuit; Hon. Leonard Garth, United States Court of Appeals, Third Circuit; Hon. Alan B. Handler, New Jersey Supreme Court; Hon. Nathan S. Heffernan, Wisconsin Supreme Court; Hon. Florence R. Peskoe, New Jersey Administrative Office of the Courts, now Judge of the Juvenile and Domestic Relations Court, Monmouth County, New Jersey; Hon. Mary Schroeder, U.S. Court of Appeals, Ninth Circuit;[5] Hon. Janie L. Shores, Alabama Supreme Court; and Mr. Irwin Stolz, of Atlanta, Georgia.

Gratefully acknowledged too are the cooperation and support received from judges, administrators, and clerical staff in each of the jurisdictions where court record and interview data were collected. These persons often not only provided access to court record data but in addition gave freely of their time by answering many questions and sharing insights about appellate court operations that would otherwise have been unobtainable. We would particularly like to acknow-

---

4. The experiments include preargument settlement programs in the Rhode Island and Connecticut Supreme Courts and in the Pennsylvania Superior Court (an intermediate court of appeals), an accelerated docket program in the Colorado Court of Appeals, and an oral decision docket in the California First District Court of Appeal. Prof. Jerry Goldman, of Northwestern University, the project evaluator, has been responsible for monitoring the experiments.

5. Judge Peskoe and Judge Schroeder served on the Advisory Board during the project's first phase, January 1978 through July 1979.

ledge the assistance provided by the following: Hon. Harry S. Silverstein, former Chief Judge, Colorado Court of Appeals; Hon. David P. Enoch, present Chief Judge, Colorado Court of Appeals; Hon. Edwin T. Ruland, Colorado Court of Appeals; Mr. Mac Danford, Clerk, Colorado Court of Appeals; Hon. Arthur England, Chief Justice, Florida Supreme Court; Hon. E. R. Mills, Chief Judge, Florida Court of Appeal, First District; Mr. Raymond Rhodes, Clerk, Florida Court of Appeal, First District; Hon. Robert Downing, Illinois Appellate Court, First District; Mr. Lee Marsh, Administrator, Illinois Appellate Court, First District; Hon. Paul Buchanan, Chief Judge, Indiana Court of Appeals; Mr. Joseph Quest, Administrator, Indiana Court of Appeals; Hon. Frank Haswell, Chief Justice, Montana Supreme Court; Mr. Gary Goff, Montana State Court Administrator's Office; Hon. Norman Krivosha, Chief Justice, Nebraska Supreme Court; Mr. Larry Donelson, Clerk, Nebraska Supreme Court; Hon. Robert Matthews, Presiding Judge for Administration, New Jersey Superior Court, Appellate Division; Hon. Milton Conford, former Presiding Judge for Administration, New Jersey Superior Court, Appellate Division; Hon. Thomas J. Parrino, Chief Judge, Ohio Court of Appeals, Eighth District; Ms. Vilma Kohn, Administrator, Ohio Court of Appeals; Eighth District; Hon. Herbert M. Schwab, Chief Judge, Oregon Court of Appeals; Mr. Douglas Bray, Oregon State Court Administrator's Office; Hon. Lawrence W. I'Anson, former Chief Justice, Virginia Supreme Court; Mr. Allen L. Lucy, Clerk, Virginia Supreme Court; and Mrs. Anne Dean, Petitions Clerk, Virginia Supreme Court.

We wish to thank several persons knowledgeable about appellate courts who reviewed the results of the project data analysis and provided insightful comments and suggestions for improving this book: Prof. Alfred Blumstein, Urban Systems Institute, Carnegie-Mellon University; Prof. Anne N. Costain, Department of Political Science, University of Colorado; Prof. Jerry Goldman, Department of Political Science, Northwestern University; and Prof. Robert A. Leflar, former Dean of the Law School, University of Arkansas, and former Associate Justice of the Arkansas Supreme Court. Statistical reviews and guidance were also provided by Mr. Roger Hall, former Director of the New Hampshire Statistical Analysis Center, and by Dr. Carolyn F. Shettle, former Director of the Massachusetts Statistical Center.

Two former members of the national Appellate Justice Improvement Project staff deserve special mention. Barry Mahoney, who served as project director during the initial nine months of the project, nurtured the project during its early stages and started it on a productive course. Steven Weller, initially a senior staff member on the project, assumed the job of director after Mr. Mahoney's departure. During his tenure as project director, Mr. Weller was largely responsible for developing and implementing the research design for collecting data incorporated in this volume.

Other National Center for State Courts personnel who have made significant contributions are Thomas B. Marvell, a senior staff attorney whose participation was instrumental in the data-collection efforts in two courts included in the study and who was coauthor of two earlier project staff studies; Samuel D. Conti, Director of the National Center's Northeastern Regional Office, for his extensive editorial review and comment; Carolyn McMurran, editor at National Center headquarters; and Gloria Colson, the project secretary.

Finally, we would like to express special thanks to four individuals who have provided support, encouragement, and guidance during the course of the project: Nicholas Demos, the project monitor from LEAA; Edward B. McConnell, Director of the National Center for State Courts; and John Greacen, Deputy Director for Programs of the National Center for State Courts.

Even though all of the above-mentioned individuals and organizations have made significant contributions, the authors assume full responsibility for the content and the opinions expressed in this document.

DECEMBER 1980

JOHN A. MARTIN
ELIZABETH A. PRESCOTT

Executive Summary

The Appellate Justice Improvement Project of the National Center for State Courts has investigated the problem of case processing delay in appellate courts within the context of the following frequently raised questions. What are the major characteristics of the different environments in which appellate courts operate? How long does it take to process cases in these different environments? When does case processing time constitute delay? How do differences in time relate to differences in case volume, case types, court organization, structure, and procedure? Can solutions to delay developed by one court be successfully adopted by other courts?

Sample Courts and Study Methods

The ten appellate courts included in the study were chosen to ensure that the final sample would reflect so far as possible the diversity of the state appellate court population. The sample courts[1] are a mix of intermediate courts and courts of last resort, from different geographic locations across the country, with differing caseloads, case processing times, procedures, and structures.

Data for the study came from three sources: library research, which provided information about the constitutional and statutory provisions and court rules that governed each court; a systematic sample of approximately 5,900 cases, filed during 1975-76; and site visits to the sample courts. The years 1975-76 were selected in order to ensure that most of the 500 cases included in each court sample would have been disposed of and hence would furnish complete time-lapse data at the time of data collection in 1978. The case-record data-collection instrument was designed to capture all the time-lapse information available in the court records, and all the relevant case characteristics that it was expected might relate to case processing time and therefore to delay.

Measuring Processing Time and Delay

Total case processing time was defined and measured as the number of days from the date of judgment in an initial forum, usually a trial

---

1. The sample courts are the Colorado Court of Appeals; the Florida First District Court of Appeal; the Illinois Appellate Court, First District; the Indiana Court of Appeals; the Montana Supreme Court; the Nebraska Supreme Court; the New Jersey Superior Court, Appellate Division; the Ohio Court of Appeals, Eighth District; the Oregon Court of Appeals; and the Virginia Supreme Court.

Executive Summary

court, to the date of issuance of the final mandate or its equivalent by the appellate court. This is not the time interval that courts themselves regard as processing time: courts ordinarily measure from the date of the filing of the appeal, which usually comes after the order or judgment below, to the date of the release of the opinion. The study used a more comprehensive time frame, representing the total time litigants are involved in appeals and thus the standard against which the courts' users measure appellate review time. In addition, this time frame emphasizes the importance of viewing the appellate process as a comprehensive system that must operate efficiently at all stages.

To describe processing time accurately and to isolate specific problems, the total period was divided into intervals corresponding to steps in the typical appellate process: Step 1, from judgment to "at issue" (i.e., when all materials necessary to decide a case have been filed, also referred to as "perfection" of the appeal); Step 2, from "at issue" to the date of submission, usually the date of oral argument; Step 3, from oral argument to decision; and Step 4, from decision to mandate.

An examination of the relative contribution of each step to the case processing time total in each court helped isolate the points where cases were being delayed. Although two courts might display similar total case processing time averages, the relative contributions of the individual steps in the process could nonetheless differ dramatically, revealing different points of delay requiring different solutions.

Defining delay was an awkward but necessary task. Delay had first to be defined in order to determine its existence, describe its prevalence, and where possible, to isolate and identify its causes. Without some objective definition, the issue of delay would remain largely one of individual perception, and thus subject to wide interpretation.

In this study the measure for determining delay is the percentage of cases in each court that exceeded the time set by the court's own rules for completing the steps in an appeal. This method of measurement is not perfect, but by using each court's own standards the problem of subjecting some courts to the biases of others was largely avoided. Each court's processing time was analyzed within the context of its own system, which included its rules. Because all courts allow time extensions, albeit with varying frequency, data for actual processing time were compared not only with the standards expressed in courts' filing rules but also with the time elapsed as a result of extensions allowed.

Principal Findings

Processing Time Diversity Among the Sample Courts

The sample courts differed dramatically in the amount of time

Appellate Court Delay

required to process cases.

Three methods of gauging time elapsed in completing appeals were employed. The first was to establish the average number of days in the full sample. Case processing time ranged from an average 240 days in the Oregon Court of Appeals to a 649-day average in the Illinois Appellate Court, First District.

Use of these data as to jurisdictionally similar courts reveals the following average processing times.

Courts of Last Resort*	Days
Nebraska Supreme Court	301
Montana Supreme Court	370
Virginia Supreme Court	484
Intermediate Appellate Courts, *Statewide Jurisdiction*	
Oregon Court of Appeals	240
New Jersey Superior Court, Appellate Division	379
Colorado Court of Appeals	431
Indiana Court of Appeals	641
Intermediate Appellate Court, *County or Regional Jurisdiction*	
Florida Court of Appeal, First District	333
Ohio Court of Appeals, Eighth District	413
Illinois Appellate Court, First District	649

None of the Courts of Last Resort are in states where there is an intermediate appellate court.

In the second statistical method, when time distributions were measured by quartiles, the degree of diversity among courts was even greater than that revealed through a simple comparison of means and medians. For example, in the Oregon Court of Appeals, 75 percent of all the cases (the third quartile) were processed in 269 days or less, or significantly faster than the bulk of cases in other courts. In the sampled Illinois intermediate appeals court, it took 799 days to dispose of the same percentage of cases.

A third technique for summarizing the differences in total case processing time between courts—that of breaking down each court's time distribution by percentage of completed cases falling within a series of six-month intervals—revealed that while the vast majority of cases in the three fastest courts were completed in a year or less after lower court judgment (90 percent in the Oregon Court of Appeals, 71 percent in the Nebraska Supreme Court, and 67 percent in the Florida Court of Appeal, First District), only about 10 percent of the cases in the slower courts were completed within the same time period. By the end of two years, most of the courts had disposed of all but a very small fraction of their total caseloads. Two courts, however, deviated substantially from this pattern: figures for the Illinois Appellate

Executive Summary

Court, First District, and the Indiana Court of Appeals revealed that nearly one-third of these courts' cases took more than two years to complete during the period of the sample.

Components of Total Case Processing Time: The Predecision Phase

The time elapsed during the first phase of the process (Step 1, lower court judgment to submission) ranged from a mean of 153 days in the Oregon Court of Appeals to a mean of 383 days in the Illinois Appellate Court, First District. Although the specific number of days attributable to the first phase of the appellate process differed from court to court, in all but one of the courts (the Ohio Court of Appeals, Eighth District) the processing time that elapsed during this phase represented the largest percentage of the total case processing time of any of the four steps, ranging from 41 percent in the Florida court to 62 percent in the New Jersey Superior Court, Appellate Division.

> Because the period between the lower court judgment and the perfection of the appeal often represents a very large percentage of the total life of an appeal, reforms designed to shorten the total processing time will often have to focus on this phase.

In many jurisdictions, the control over the preparation of appellate case documents traditionally has not been exercised by the appellate court, but rather by trial court judges, administrators, and litigants' attorneys. Efficient case processing, however, may require that appellate court judges in those jurisdictions oversee and discharge more administrative duties, and assume a broader managerial and supervisory role than that to which they are accustomed.

> While the courts (although jurisdictionally varied) differed only moderately in the time specified in their rules for filing appellate materials (from 120 to 195 days), they differed dramatically in their adherence to those standards as evidenced by the wide range of the percentage of cases exceeding court rules.

In only two of the courts included in the sample, Virginia and Oregon, were a majority of the appeals processed within the time limitations established by court rules. Using the strictest definition, one could conclude that the bulk of cases in the other courts were delayed. Such a definition of delay may be unrealistic because it does not account for the possibility that in some cases there may be a legitimate need for time extensions. It may also be criticized as allowing the eradication of delay simply by elongating rule periods without reference to standards of what constitutes reasonable processing time for court users. If the standard is modified by the addition of one 30-day extension, the percentage of cases exceeding that standard is smaller and continues to decrease when two extensions are allowed

Appellate Court Delay

(one for the appellant, for example, and one for the appellee), and decreases further when three extensions are allowed. It is doubtful, however, that many cases are so complex that they legitimately require this much time beyond that automatically allowed by the court's rules.

Differences in processing time among courts for Step 2 of the appellate process—elapsed time between "at issue" and oral argument—are even greater than differences for the materials-preparation phase, Step 1. Average times ranged from a low of 27 days in the Oregon Court of Appeals to nearly ten times as much, 266 days, in the Ohio Court of Appeals, Eighth District. Only two other courts besides the Oregon Court, the Nebraska and Montana Supreme Courts, had waiting period averages at this stage of less than 100 days.

For Step 2, there were no rule standards in the courts studied against which to compare the data. Consequently, a hypothetical standard of 60 days was selected for comparative purposes. Using this measure, only one court (the Oregon Court of Appeals) would have heard a majority of its cases within that time. If an additional 30 days were allowed, two more courts (Nebraska and Montana) would have heard the bulk of their cases. If 90 days were added to the hypothetical standard (for a total of 150 days, or about five months), all courts but one would have heard most of their cases.

> A long waiting time between "at issue" and oral argument has serious secondary effects on the court system, affecting, among other things, materials-preparation time. The data suggest that when a court is unable to consider appeals promptly, as they become perfected, that court is more likely to grant extensions during the preparation phase. This, in turn, very likely acts as a disincentive for lower court clerks, court reporters, and attorneys to file materials promptly.

The Decision-Making Phase

Although the average times for the decision phase differed among the courts examined, the magnitude of the differences in Step 3 of the appellate process (time elapsed between the date of oral argument and decision announcement) was very small when compared to the large differences in the courts' predecision phases. Specifically, the processing time attributable to Step 3 fell within the relatively narrow range of 24 days on the average in the Oregon Court of Appeals to an average of 74 days in the Indiana Court of Appeals. Translating the day averages into percentages of total case processing time revealed a relatively uniform picture—between 6 and 17 percent of the courts' total case processing times were used in the decision phase, Step 3.

There were no rules in these courts specifying how quickly after oral argument opinions should be announced. However, the American Bar

Executive Summary

Association's standards for appellate courts[2] do provide a comparative measure of 60 to 90 days.

> Compared with ABA standards, all the sample courts decided at least a majority of their cases before the expiration of the maximum time suggested (either 60 or 90 days). When an additional 90 days are added to the standard, for a total of 150 to 180 days after argument, six of the courts had decided over 95 percent of their cases within the standard; the Indiana court had the greatest percentage of cases still outstanding (16 percent).

Finally, substantial differences existed among the courts regarding the average amount of time elapsed between decision announcement and mandate issuance, Step 4. The average processing times attributable to the final step ranged from a low of 6 days for non-oral-argument cases in the Montana Supreme Court to a high of 130 days for oral-argument cases in the Indiana Court of Appeals. The range, when expressed as a percentage of the total case processing time, was between 3 and 21 percent.

A hypothetical standard of 30 days was devised for examining Step 4, decision to mandate. In New Jersey, where the opinion itself serves as the mandate, there is no lapse of time, although counsel may file a motion for a stay within ten days of the entry of the appellate judgment. When measured against this standard, half of the courts had completed the step for the majority of their cases within that time, and half exceeded it for most of their cases. After 90 days had elapsed, all the courts had closed most of their cases. However, in three courts (Colorado, Indiana, and Illinois), a significant percentage of cases (18 percent, 22 percent, and 29 percent, respectively) were not completed even after 120 days had elapsed.

> In all of the appellate courts included in this study, at least a few cases exceeded the time limitations specified in court rules at some stage of the appellate process. Those delays can be viewed as case-specific or idiosyncratic exceptions within generally efficient court systems. In some courts, however, the time limitations were exceeded routinely at specific stages, and in a few courts the majority of all the cases exceeded processing time standards at all stages of the appellate process. Delays of the latter type do not reflect mere idiosyncratic by-products, but rather indicate potentially serious systemic problems.

Volume and Delay

Much of the extensive current literature extolling the virtues of one

---

2. American Bar Association Commission on Standards of Judicial Administration, *Standards Relating to Appellate Courts* (Chicago: American Bar Association, 1977).

appellate reform or another is predicated on the assumption that the problems of increasing case volume and of increasing appellate court delay are inextricably bound together.[3] That is, many observers make the assumption that the greater a court's caseload, the longer it will take to dispose of cases. The present analysis of relationships between case volume, case processing time, and delay suggests, however, that volume has been overemphasized as the primary source of appellate court delay and that the relation between volume and delay is a subtle one.

This examination of the relationship between volume, case processing time, and delay used two measures of volume. First, the absolute number of filings per year was considered. The second measure was the number of filings per judge. The use of both measures yielded some interesting and somewhat perplexing findings.

> There was found to be a very slight tendency for total case processing time and the percentage of cases exceeding court rules to increase in a positive relation to the absolute case volume among the sample courts. There was, moreover, a moderate to strong tendency for case processing time and delay to *decrease* as the number of filings per judge increased.

In other words, courts with larger caseloads took no longer or only slightly longer to process their cases than did courts with smaller caseloads; and courts with more filings per judge were even appreciably faster than courts with relatively fewer cases per judge. The same trend is observed when the four different steps in the appellate process are examined individually, with one important exception—a moderate to strong positive relationship between volume and Step 2 time ("at issue" to oral argument) regardless of the measure of volume used: as total filings or filings per judge increase, waiting time at Step 2, which reflects case backlog, also increases. We conclude that the amount of backlog in a given court is not, however, totally a function of volume, but rather is a function of the complex interplay of volume, decision-making efficiency, and managerial style. Some courts simply hear and decide cases more quickly than do others. Nevertheless, those courts that decide cases more quickly are not necessarily those with fewer cases to decide. On the contrary, the data analysis showed that decision time decreased as volume increased among the sample courts, regardless of the measure of volume.

This analysis, however, does not lead to the conclusion that case volume is unimportant. An increase in case volume can jeopardize the speed with which a court disposes of its caseload, requiring adjustments especially in courts experiencing sudden and substantial

---

3. *See generally* Paul Carrington, Daniel Meador, and Maurice Rosenberg, *Justice on Appeal* (St. Paul: West Publishing Co., 1976).

Executive Summary

increases in case volumes. The lack of a general positive relationship between case volume and delay in the sample courts also does not mean that there is no correlation between volume and delay or no upper limits on how many cases courts can effectively process, even if compensatory organizational, procedural, and structural adjustments are made; however, those upper limits appear not to have been reached in the courts studied. These findings may thus give rise to a certain amount of optimism: they suggest that appellate courts are not totally at the mercy of seemingly ever increasing caseloads, phenomena over which they have little or no direct control.

Case Types

Analysis of relationships between case types, case processing time, and delay focused on answering two related questions.[4] First, do differences in case type and case characteristics[5] correlate with differences in case processing time within each of the sample courts? Second, if there are significant relationships between case types and characteristics and processing time within a jurisdiction, are the patterns of relationships consistent across jurisdictions, i.e., are the case types that require longer processing the same from one court to another?

> Case processing time and delay did not vary according to the parties and attorneys involved in appeals, or the substantive content of appeals, matters over which appellate courts have little or no control. The lack of systematic variations was apparent both within the courts studied and among them. In the few instances where differences were discernible in processing time among some categories of cases, they were isolated, occurring in only one court, or at most in a few courts.

These findings suggest that the differences in the configurations of the caseloads confronting appellate courts have little or no effect on the time required to process cases. It would appear that virtually any case can at least potentially be disposed of within reasonable time limitations, regardless of the parties involved or the jurisprudential content of the appeal.

---

4. To determine whether differences among variable category means were statistically significant, F tests were performed for each nominal-level case characteristic variable. Spearman's rho was used for ordinal-level variables and Pearson's r for interval-level variables.

5. The following case-characteristic variables were included in the analysis: type of appellant and appellee, status of parties in lower court, type of attorneys, total number of appellants and number of appellees, case subject matter(s), appeal issue(s), number of subject matters, number of issues, source of appeal, brief lengths, transcript and record lengths, number and content of motions, opinion types and lengths.

Appellate Court Delay

The analysis, however, did reveal positive relationships, both within and among courts, among the average number of extensions per case, brief and opinion lengths, and processing time and delay. These aspects of the appellate process can be controlled by appellate courts themselves, through enforcement of policies on extensions and on opinion and brief length.

The Roots of Appellate Court Delay: Structure, Organization, and Procedures

The structures and procedures of appellate courts appear to have a greater impact on the time it takes them to process their cases than do the number or type of cases filed.

This is an optimistic conclusion. Structure and procedure, unlike case volume or type, may be controlled by the courts themselves, and may therefore be modified or altered by court personnel. More specifically, the project made a number of significant observations.

1. Standards specifying the amount of time to complete the initial steps in the appellate process (i.e., filing notices of appeal, briefs, records, and transcripts) are important correlates of case processing time. The analysis revealed strong positive relationships between the number of days specified in court rules and elapsed actual days, for both total case processing time and predecision time intervals. As the number of days specified in court rules increased, processing time also increased; court rules themselves may create an expectation of what constitutes case processing time and delay.

2. Policies specifying which court or courts control time extensions have an impact on predecision case processing time. Where authority for granting all time extensions rests exclusively in the appellate court, predecision processing time is substantially reduced. The relatively slowest appellate systems were those in which authority to grant extensions overlapped—where time extensions for a single step in the appellate process, i.e., to file records, could be granted by both trial and appellate courts, first by one and then by the other.

The presence or absence of procedures to screen or sort cases prior to judicial considerations, e.g., by central staff, correlated neither positively nor negatively with case processing time.

3. There is no single "best way" to organize decision-making power. Courts that are divided into panels, for example, are not necessarily any faster or slower than courts that hear cases en banc. In addition, the analysis revealed no systematic relationships between case processing time and either the number of panels, or the number of judges per panel, or whether the panels have rotating memberships.

Executive Summary

The analysis did indicate that the courts that had formal conflict-resolution mechanisms—e.g., conferences bringing the court's members together to consider opinions prepared by each panel—generally had substantially shorter decision time averages than did those courts that did not have these mechanisms.

4. Courts that used summary disposition techniques generally had shorter decision time averages. Although the specific techniques varied from court to court, the element common to all successful summary disposition techniques appears to be whether or not they bypassed steps in the traditional appellate process, e.g., oral argument or written opinions.

Directions for Future Appellate Court Reform

State appellate courts are not wholly at the mercy of seemingly ever-increasing caseloads. When necessary, courts can modify their structure and organization or adjust their procedures to meet the demands of larger caseloads.

Workable solutions to delay are available. However, each appellate court is in many ways a unique system. No single solution or set of solutions will necessarily solve every court's problems. Solutions must be developed within the context of a particular court's goals, needs, structure, and organization.

Meaningful and effective appellate reform will require courts to approach an old problem with a fresh perspective. It will require appellate courts to undertake considerable self-examination, to experiment with a variety of possible delay-reducing techniques, and to evaluate rigorously the consequences of the techniques with which they have experimented and to be prepared to abandon approaches found unsuitable. Perhaps most important, meaningful reform will require judges, administrators, lawyers, legislators, and citizens to be committed to a philosophy of experimentation, evaluation, modification and change.

An Introduction to This Study 1

Court delay is much more than a statistical curiosity, a popular topic of the media, or a seemingly mandatory agenda item at many professional conferences. Litigation may alter permanently the lives of the parties directly involved as well as those of other members of society. Appellate courts often determine irrevocably whether a person will be compensated for injury or loss, or released from confinement or continued in incarceration. These courts may help to determine the direction and scope of important public policy. When the resolution of appeals is delayed, lives may be disrupted while individuals and society, unable because of the delay to plan confidently for the future, await the final disposition of cases.

Though commentators have differed in their assessments of the impact of delay on litigants, judges, and court personnel, it is generally agreed that court delay compromises the quality of justice. This conclusion is based, implicitly, on the premise that the speedy resolution of controversies is a fundamental societal goal which, with alarming frequency, is not being met by the courts. A recent survey of public opinion about the judicial system revealed that commentators apparently are not alone in embracing this assumption: a substantial percentage of those surveyed among the general public also viewed court delay as a serious problem.[1]

Responding to these concerns, the Appellate Justice Improvement Project based its research on the assumption that the speedy resolution of cases is a desirable societal goal. Project staff recognized, however, that appellate courts have other important and concurrent goals, such as making correct decisions, maintaining public access to the courts, ensuring litigants' procedural protections, and preparing opinions of appropriate quality. As a consequence, the issue of delay was examined to the fullest extent practicable in light of the multiple needs and goals of particular appellate systems. This perspective is reflected in the following questions for which the project sought answers and which are addressed in this study.

---

1. Yankelovich, Skelly, and White, Inc. *The Public Image of the Courts: Highlights of a National Survey of the General Public, Judges, Lawyers, and Community Leaders* (Williamsburg, Va.: National Center for State Courts, 1978).

2 *Appellate Court Delay*

Questions Investigated

What are the characteristics of the environments in which state appellate courts operate?

Aspects of the court environment that may affect case processing time include the constitutional and statutory provisions that define the legal structure of a court, the size of the population served by it, the geographic location of the court and its personnel, the workload as defined by annual filings and case inventory, and the resources available to the court, e.g., the size of its operating budget, the type of recordkeeping facilities it uses, and the number of judges and support personnel.

An understanding of a court's rules and procedures is crucial to assessing the existence, potential sources, and severity of delay. Rules may serve as benchmarks for assessing the performance of a court: Are the participants meeting the time requirements set by court rules?

How long does it take to process cases in various appellate court environments?

The total case processing time in each sample court was divided into a series of time intervals corresponding to steps in the appellate process. The results of this analysis appear in Chapter 3, which presents the average case processing times for each time interval, as well as information concerning the degree of time variation among cases within a particular court and among courts.

When does case processing time constitute delay?

Determining when case processing time can be labeled delay presupposes that delay can be defined and measured. Often, the determination of whether or not the amount of time required to process a given case constitutes delay is a perceptual matter. Consequently, Chapter 3 attempts to provide a working definition of delay and to show how it was applied in the study, and then reports the amount of delay (as so defined) which the analysis indicated existed in each of the sample courts at the time of the surveyed cases.

How do differences in case processing time relate to differences in case volume, case types, court organization, and court procedures?

Once a determination has been made that delay exists and the degree of delay has been measured, the next logical step is to identify what are and what are not its sources. In an effort to identify those sources, Chapter 4 examines the relationship between case types and processing time and between volume and processing time; and Chapters 5 and 6 examine organizational and procedural features of courts and processing time.

How may courts successfully implement the various techniques currently being advanced to solve the problems of appellate court delay?

Chapter 7 offers general conclusions, presents arguments in favor of appellate systems' adopting incremental delay-reduction strategies, and outlines the principal components of such a strategy.

Information Sources

Three types of information are incorporated in this study: (1) descriptive information about the constitutional provisions, statutes, and court rules that define court jurisdiction and organizational structure and that loosely govern operations in each of the ten sample courts; (2) case record data from a systematic sample of 5,900 cases, filed during 1975 and 1976,[2] and (3) information on court problems and operations gained from interviews with judges and court personnel in each court.

The Ten Sample Courts

The courts comprising the sample were chosen to provide diversity in several key aspects, among them caseload, reported case processing time, and geographic location. (See Tables 1-1 and 1-2.)

The courts are alike in one important respect: all are courts of first appellate jurisdiction, i.e., none of the states in which the three supreme courts sit have intermediate appellate courts.

---

2. These years were chosen to ensure that most cases would be closed by the time of data collection (June-July, 1978).

TABLE 1-1
Jurisdictional Characteristics of the Sample Courts

Court	Approximate Population Served	Geographic Jurisdiction	Permanent Location	Oral Argument Location(s)
New Jersey Superior Court, Appellate Division	7,200,000	entire state	Trenton	Newark, Hackensack, Trenton
Virginia Supreme Court	4,700,000	entire state	Richmond	Richmond, Portsmouth, Roanoke*
Florida Court of Appeal, First District	1,800,000	northern and panhandle parts of state	Tallahassee	Circuit court headquarters within the district.
Ohio Court of Appeals, Eighth District	1,725,000	Cuyahoga County	Cleveland	Cleveland
Indiana Court of Appeals	5,200,000	entire state	Indianapolis	Indianapolis**
Illinois Appellate Court, First District	5,500,000	Cook County	Chicago	Chicago
Nebraska Supreme Court	1,500,000	entire state	Lincoln	Lincoln
Montana Supreme Court	700,000	entire state	Helena	Helena
Colorado Court of Appeals	2,200,000	entire state	Denver	Denver
Oregon Court of Appeals	2,100,000	entire state	Salem	Salem

*For oral argument on petitions. Once the petition has been granted, oral argument on the appeal is held in Richmond only. Also, Roanoke was discontinued as a site for petition oral arguments in 1979.

**Some arguments have been held at locations within the first and third districts of the court. This, however, is unusual, arguments being scheduled out-state for ceremonial purposes only.

TABLE 1-2
Caseloads of Courts Included in the Study

Court	No. of Judges 1975-76	No. of Filings 1975	No. of Filings 1976	No. of Filings Per Judge 1975	No. of Filings Per Judge 1976
New Jersey Superior Court, Appellate Division	21	4,339	4,819	207	230
Virginia Supreme Court	7	1,526	1,672	218	239
Florida District Court of Appeal, First District	5	1,664	1,875	333	375
Ohio Court of Appeals, Eighth District	6	1,701	1,720	284	287
Indiana Court of Appeals	9	626	777	70	86
Illinois Appellate Court, First District	20	1,942	1,731	97	86
Nebraska Supreme Court	7	571	615	82	88
Montana Supreme Court	5	299	409	60	82
Colorado Court of Appeals	10	858	915	86	92
Oregon Court of Appeals	6	1,539	1,847	256	308

2 Appellate Delay and Court Reform

Previous studies have dealt extensively with the sources of delay in appellate courts and in courts generally. These studies have suggested a myriad of responses available to courts challenged by expanding caseloads and unacceptable case processing times. Although the scope of prior efforts to identify the loci of delay has varied, these studies have, for the most part, isolated three possible sources:

Caseload Appellate courts simply do not have the personnel or resources to keep up with increasing case volumes.[1]

Inefficiency Judges and other appellate court personnel do not use their time effectively. Courts are poorly organized and inadequately administered. Even if appellate court resources were increased, litigants would still encounter substantial delay in case processing time.[2]

A combination of caseload and inefficiency There are too many cases, and courts lack sufficient resources and are poorly

---

1. See, for example, Carrington, Meador, and Rosenberg, *Justice on Appeal* (St. Paul, Minn.: West Publishing Co., 1976); "Alabama Appellate Court Congestion: Observations, and Suggestions from an Empirical Study," *Alabama Law Review* 150 (1968); Baker, Watkins, Lardy, "Appellate Court Reform," 45 *Mississippi Law Journal* 121 (1974); Paul D. Carrington, "Crowded Dockets and the Court of Appeal," 52 *Harvard Law Review* 542 (1969); Cartwright, Friedman, and Wheeler, "The Business of State Supreme Courts," 30 *Stanford Law Review* 121 (1977); "Judicial Statistics of State Courts of Last Resort," 31 *Journal of the American Judicature Society* (1947); and Albert Tate, Jr., "Containing the Law Explosion," 56 *Judicature* 228 (1973).

2. Proponents of this position include the following: Harry Jones, ed., *The Courts, the Public, and the Law Explosion* (Englewood Cliffs: Prentice-Hall, 1965); Ziesel, Kalven, and Buchholz, *Delay in the Court* (Boston: Little, Brown, 1959); "Appellate Case Management and Decisional Processes," 61 *Virginia Law Review* 225 (1975); R. E. English, "Crisis in Civil Appeals," 50 *Chicago Bar Record* 231 (1969); Donald Hunter, "Riding the Circuit: Indiana Probes Delay," 59 *Judicature* 18 (1975-76); Jacobson and Schroeder, "Arizona's Experiment with Appellate Reform," 63 *American Bar Association Journal* 1226 (1977); Robert Leflar, "Appellate Judicial Innovation," 27 *Oklahoma Law Review* 321 (1974); Kenneth J. O'Connell, "Streamlining Appellate Procedures," 56 *Judicature* 234 (1973); Sulelan and Spencer, "Constitutional Relief for an Overburdened Court," 8 *William and Mary Law Review* 244 (1967); Editorial, "Ways to Relieve Appellate Court Congestion," 56 *Judicature* 94 (1973); and K.C. Todd, "Appellate Delay in the Criminal Courts of Texas," 37 *Texas Bar Journal* 454 (1974).

organized and administered.[3]

As might be expected, solutions suggested by various authorities to the problems of delay and volume are directly related to those authorities' perceptions of the sources of delay. Yet even though judges and other persons concerned about improving appellate courts may be aware of many if not most currently proposed delay-reduction solutions, the previous literature has offered surprisingly few guidelines to help courts determine which solutions may work given the specific but varying needs of particular appellate systems. The literature has not offered a comprehensive conceptual overview of the multiple dimensions of delay and therefore of the solutions proposed for reducing it. This volume attempts to provide a conceptual framework for classifying solutions to the problems of appellate court volume and delay.

A Conceptual Framework for Classifying Solutions

Figure 2-1 presents a two-dimensional framework for categorizing proposed solutions to court delay. The first dimension divides perspectives on court reform between (1) those emphasizing large case volume as the primary source of appellate court delay, and (2) those emphasizing inefficiency as the primary source of delay. The second classifying dimension divides solutions between (a) those that emphasize reducing delay by adding resources and (b) those that emphasize reducing delay by restructuring the use of existing court resources.

Solutions based on row A (Types I and II) are volume directed. Though they may differ from one another in the degree to which they emphasize the importance of case volume as the primary correlate of case processing time, they are typically designed to decrease the ratio of cases to personnel. These solutions are predicated on the assumption that if the ratio of personnel to cases is increased, the amount of time required to process cases will decrease.

In contrast, solutions in row B (Types III and IV) are more specifically efficiency directed. Solutions of these types, unlike volume-directed solutions, do not proceed from the assumption that large case volume is the primary source of delay or that volume is the key to diminishing delay. Though efficiency-directed solutions recognize the importance of volume, they emphasize addressing processing time or delay directly. These techniques usually focus on using new

---

3. Examples of this position are numerous. Comprehensive assessments include Osthus and Shapiro, *Congestion and Delay in State Appellate Courts* (Chicago: American Judicature Society, 1974); John Reed, *The Applications of Operations Research to Court Delay* (New York: Praeger, 1973); the results of a symposium, "Judges on Appellate Reform," 23 *UCLA Law Review* 419 (1976), and Richard Record, Jr., "Remedies for Backlog in the Appellate Court of Illinois," 62 *Illinois Bar Journal* 82 (1973).

FIGURE 2-1
A Framework for Classifying Solutions to Court Delay

	Adding Resources	Restructuring Resources
A Volume-Directed	**TYPE I** Emphasis: There are too many cases or not enough person-power to handle increased filings effectively. The goal of reform is to decrease the ratio of cases to personnel by adding more personnel. In turn delay will be reduced. All cases will receive similar consideration.	**TYPE II** Emphasis: There are many cases, but they can be handled if existing resources are used more selectively. All cases do not merit similar consideration. The goal of reform is to indirectly decrease the ratio of cases to personnel by restructuring the use of existing personnel and resources. In turn, delay will be reduced.
B Efficiency-Directed	**TYPE III** Emphasis: Regardless of how many cases there are, they *all* must be processed efficiently. Delay must be attacked directly. Courts are not efficient and need to add new time-saving technologies. The goal of reform is to reduce delay in all cases. All cases will benefit from the application of modern technology.	**TYPE IV** Emphasis: All cases must be processed more efficiently. Delay must be attacked directly by implementing efficient rules and procedures. The goal of reform is to reduce delay in all cases. All cases will benefit from the application of efficient procedures.

technologies or procedural changes to reduce processing time for all cases during some phases or to eliminate or streamline some steps in the traditional appellate process.

In Figure 2-2, solutions in column A are predicated on courts' obtaining additional funds to hire more personnel or to develop new technologies:

> When all is considered, there is little that can be done about volume. The tide of affairs which produces litigation and appeals is largely beyond our control.... In the end, if appellate justice is to be provided, there is no alternative to the erection of a judicial system of a size sufficient to accommodate the needs of all citizens seeking just decisions.[4]

In contrast, column B solutions emphasizes the need for courts to restructure their use of existing resources with an eye toward increased productivity, rather than to add more resources as volume increases. When the two dimensions (the volume-delay dimension, and the resource dimension) are combined, they form the two-by-two matrix presented in Figure 2-2. The four separate cells are here labeled Types I, II, III, IV.

A Brief Critique of Proposed Solutions

Using the Figure 2-2 framework, this section will classify and briefly analyze some of the more popular proposed solutions to the problems of appellate court volume and delay. The list of proposed solutions examined is not exhaustive. Comprehensive literature reviews are already available, and it is not necessary to replicate outstanding prior efforts.[5] Rather, it is our intention to present a fresh perspective for organizing thinking about appellate court reform, using some of the more popular proposed solutions as examples (see Figure 2-2).

Type I Solutions

The most extreme Type I solution is that of creating a new appellate court, that is, the addition of an intermediate court to a previously single-tiered appellate system. Establishing intermediate appellate courts will result, at least initially, in decreased case processing time for cases where there is only one appeal, but the long-range effects of adding new courts have only recently been explored.[6] Moreover,

---

4. Carrington et al., *Justice on Appeal,* supra note 1, at 136.
5. See, e.g., Stephen L. Wasby, et al., *Volume and Delay in State Appellate Courts: Problems and Responses* (Williamsburg, Va.: National Center for State Courts, 1979) and Robert A. Leflar, *Internal Operating Procedures of Appellate Courts* (Chicago: American Bar Foundation, 1976).
6. Victor Eugene Flango and Nora F. Blair, "Creating an intermediate appellate court: Does it reduce the caseload of a state's highest court?" 64 *Judicature* 74 (1980).

FIGURE 2-2
Proposed Solutions to Court Delay

	—A— Adding Resources	—B— Restructuring Resources
Volume-Directed	**TYPE I** Add intermediate court(s). Add judges. Add administrators. Add law clerks. Add court reporters.	**TYPE II** Increase discretionary jurisdiction. Use preargument settlement conferences. Assign cases to different processing tracks. Use panels. Hold fewer oral arguments. Use memos, orders, and unpublished opinions. Reassign cases if a judge falls behind. Use an accelerated docket.
Delay-Directed	**TYPE III** Add computer case tracking. Add other technological innovations, such as cassette recordings of lower court proceedings, automated legal research, computer-assisted transcription (CAT).	**TYPE IV** Use affirmative case management techniques, such as NOA filed in appellate court, all extensions granted only by appellate court, close monitoring of case progress, strict sanctions of those who abuse the process. Reduce filing time limits. Reduce allowable page limits of briefs. Shorten oral argument. Prepare generally shorter opinions.

adding an intermediate appellate court is an expensive and potentially long-term commitment, which may reduce the court system's willingness to try other approaches. The added costs alone in a time of budget tightening may prevent states from exercising this option.

A second Type I solution, that of adding personnel (more judges, law clerks, and administrative staff), has been a frequently exercised option for reducing appellate delay. This approach obviously assumes that if the number of cases per judicial staff member is reduced, case processing time will at least stabilize, if not decrease. Perhaps this would be true if all appellate systems were identical in structure and organization and operated under the same procedures. If that were so, adding personnel might be the most appropriate response to delay. However, various appellate courts may in many respects be more structurally, organizationally, and procedurally dissimilar than they are similar. Data examined in this study suggest that the relative number of personnel available to process cases does not necessarily determine case processing time: "faster" courts were not those with proportionally more judges, law clerks, or administrative personnel.

Additionally, the problems of integrating new personnel into an existing appellate system, the expense of new judges and their support personnel (additional offices, courtrooms, and library space) and potential political opposition from other units of government might argue against this alternative even if its application could automatically reduce delay.

Type II Solutions

The Type II category encompasses a variety of proposed delay-reduction techniques. While the scope of specific techniques may vary, they all emphasize that elapsed case processing time can be reduced if the use of resources is restructured to increase efficiency. This may be done by selecting cases for different types of consideration.

Transferring some classes of appeals from mandatory to discretionary jurisdiction is in a narrow sense a volume-directed solution aimed at redeploying resources. It does reflect the Type II emphasis summarized in Figure 2-1. In a more general sense, such a jurisdictional change has traditionally accompanied the creation of an intermediate appellate court: appeals of right are then submitted to the intermediate court, with discretionary review thereafter to the state court of last resort. This may be a good method for distributing cases more equally among units in a single appellate system. It of course does not eliminate cases. All appeals must still be processed somewhere within the system, if not by the supreme court, then by the intermediate court.

In any event, supreme courts with broad discretionary authority can reduce their caseloads. The elapsed time for processing the remaining cases, however, might not be appreciably reduced merely because there are fewer cases to decide. This would be so particularly in jurisdictions where the caseload of the supreme court is pared to those cases that are deemed to require decision in a forum of highest visibility. The available evidence does not suggest that appellate systems with supreme courts exercising broad discretionary authority process cases any faster—when those cases that are processed by the intermediate level courts are included—than do appellate systems that do not have this feature.

A second Type II solution, the preargument settlement conference procedure, is an attempt by courts to encourage the early settlement, hence disposition, of some appeals. By disposing of these cases early, preferably in the first step of the appellate process, the procedure can reduce both the number of cases that require full court consideration and the amount of resources expended on those cases. The desired result is decreased processing time both for cases that settle and for those that proceed through the entire traditional appellate process. This result, however, can only be realized if cases do indeed settle. If cases are not settled, they must proceed through the normal processing sequence. This may be especially important in those courts that suspend transcript and brief preparation until after the settlement conference is held; in those courts, the disposition time for cases failing to settle may actually be greater than it would have been had the normal court routine been followed from the beginning. Also, where there are scheduling difficulties, conferences themselves may be postponed for a considerable time.

Note that the effects of settlement procedures in state courts are relatively untested. Rigorously controlled, methodologically sound assessments of the benefits and drawbacks of settlement programs established by the Appellate Justice Improvement Project are only now being performed.[7]

A third Type II solution, differentiated case processing techniques on "fast tracks," is really a myriad of techniques developed by courts to help them hear and decide cases more rapidly. For example, one technique, summary disposition, is usually employed within the context of a system of case screening (often by a central staff attorney unit), which selects cases suitable for such disposition.[8] Summary

---

7. See "Memorandum to Appellate Justice Improvement Project Advisory Board Members," Michael J. Hudson, Project Director, in *Appellate Justice Improvement Project—Collected Papers,* ed. Michael J. Hudson (North Andover, Mass., National Center for State Courts, Northeastern Regional Office, 1981).

8. Following are some references pertinent to this subject:

Meador, Daniel J. *Appellate Courts: Staff and Process in the Crisis of Volume.* St. Paul: West Publication Co., 1974.

Farer, Tom J. and Cynthia M. Jacob. "The Appellate Process and Staff Research Attorneys in the Appellate Division of the New Jersey Superior Court: A Report of the Appellate Justice Project of the National Center for State Courts." Denver, 1974.

Ciancia, James J. "The Appellate Process and Staff Research Attorneys in the Appellate Division of the New Jersey Superior Court: A Report of the Appellate Justice

disposition has been used by courts to dispose rapidly of selected criminal appeals, especially so-called *Anders* cases (*Anders* v. *California,* 386 U.S. 738, 18 L. Ed *2d* 493, 87 S Ct. 1396) and prison disciplinary actions. Summary disposition techniques reduce substantially or eliminate one or more steps in the traditional appellate process. Typically, courts will summarily deny oral argument to selected cases, or dispose of appeals without written opinion, that is, by order or oral decision.[9]

These techniques are subject to the criticism that they lower the quality of justice that should be available to citizens. Some judges, even in courts where they are used, are uncertain of their appropriateness. A likely source of the uncertainty is that it is difficult to measure the quality of judicial work objectively. Without reliable measures of quality, it is impossible to determine whether or not summary dispositions are comparable in quality to decisions rendered through more traditional mechanisms. The issue of quality clearly merits considerable future study.

The use of accelerated docket programs is another Type II solution and may be considered a Type IV solution as well. The primary objective of these programs is to dispose of more appeals and to dispose of them more rapidly by requiring shorter records and briefs and by limiting oral argument. A secondary objective is to resolve appeals at reduced costs to litigants. The Colorado Court of Appeals' accelerated docket provides a good example of these programs.

In the Colorado Court of Appeals, an accelerated docket program has been applied to civil cases either where a transcript is deemed unnessary or where the transcript is not more than twenty-five pages

---

Project of the National Center for State Courts, 1973-1974, Second Year of the Project." Denver, 1975.

Lucas, Jo Desha. "The Appellate Process and Staff Research Attorneys in the Illinois Appellate Court: A Report of the Appellate Justice Project of the National Center for State Courts." Denver, 1974, 1975.

O'Connor, John M. "The Appellate Process and Staff Research Attorneys in the Illinois Appellate Court: A Report of the Appellate Justice Project of the National Center for State Courts, 1973-1974." Denver, 1975.

Lake, James A. "The Appellate Process and Staff Research Attorneys in the Supreme Court of Nebraska: A Report of the Appellate Justice Project of the National Center for State Courts, 1973-1974." Denver, 1974.

Lilly, Graham C. "The Appellate Process and Staff Research Attorneys in the Supreme Court of Virginia: A Report of the Appellate Justice Project of the National Center for State Courts, 1972-1973." Denver, 1974.

Lilly, Graham C. "The Appellate Process and Staff Research Attorneys in the Supreme Court of Virginia: A Report of the Appellate Justice Project of the National Center for State Courts, 1972-1973." Denver, 1974.

Oskman, G. Timothy. "The Appellate Process and Staff Research Attorneys in the Supreme Court of Virginia." Denver, 1974.

9. See Hon. David P. Enoch, Chief Judge, Colorodo Court of Appeals, Transcribed comments, December 2, 1980, in *Appellate Justice Improvement Project—Collected Papers,* ed. Michael J. Hudson, supra note 7.

long.[10] Assignment to the accelerated docket significantly changes the time requirements during the predecision phase. For example, the opening brief is due within fifteen days of the filing of the short record and the answer brief fifteen days later. A reply brief, if any, is due within five days. Briefs are also shorter; no opening or answer brief may exceed twenty pages. Finally, the program also changes time standards for the decision phase of the appellate process. If the case is accelerated, the court will usually request that counsel waive oral argument, although some limited argument may be granted. The court attempts to render decisions and waive opinions within thirty days after argument.

Type III Solutions

The Type III category embraces technological innovations or tools expressly designed to help courts more rapidly, effectively, and inexpensively process their entire caseloads, not merely to select certain cases, as is the emphasis in Type II solutions.[11] Type III solutions assume that courts are essentially integrated systems for handling information, that is, they assume that courts are systems designed to receive, process, file, analyze, and communicate information.

Computerized case tracking is one example of a Type III solution. Typically, courts will record the dates when case materials, such as records and briefs, should be filed and use the computers' information retrieval capabilities as a daily tickler to identify cases in which materials are pending or overdue. Other Type III examples may be computer-assisted transcription (CAT), a system designed to prepare and transmit more rapidly the lower court transcripts; word processing equipment to prepare, revise, and in some courts, reproduce more rapidly and effectively the court opinions; and automated legal research (principally Lexis and Westlaw).

Problems can occur when new technologies are introduced into appellate courts. The initial costs involved in obtaining new tools may be considerable; more substantial still are the costs of obtaining and training personnel to operate and maintain the system. Moreover, courts at times may acquire technology simply for the sake of having it. Advocates of courts' adopting such systems argue that the costs involved in obtaining additional equipment can be justified, in the long run, if equipment is selected on the basis of previously identified needs and is then used properly. They stress that new technology should only be introduced when it will result in doing existing tasks more

---

10. See M. Danford, "Improvements in the Colorado Court of Appeals Docket Program," 1 *App. Court Ad. Rev.* 15 (1979), and John A. Martin and Elizabeth A. Prescott, "The Problem of Delay in the Colorado Court of Appeals," 58 *Denver Law Journal* 1 (1980).
11. Associate Justice Donald P. Smith, Jr., of the Colorado Court of Appeals, provided many helpful comments concerning the use of technology in courts.

efficiently, rapidly, or cost effectively; or when it will enable courts to perform needed tasks they have previously been unable to accomplish.

Type IV Solutions

Type IV solutions (generally, affirmative case management) include a number of techniques designed to ensure that courts process cases promptly. Several features of such a management system deserve particular mention. First, such a system requires effective caseload monitoring, i.e., techniques for identifying the progress both of specific cases and of the entire caseload during all phases of the appellate process. Case tracking enables a court to identify rapidly those cases that are overdue in some respect and also provides information to be used in periodic evaluations of the system's effectiveness. Failure by attorneys to act may even, in some systems, trigger automatic dismissal without further clerical or judicial review. Second, a program for affirmative case management requires the clear articulation and enforcement of the rules governing the filing of all case documents—notices of appeal, records, transcripts, and briefs. The appellate court assumes all authority to grant time extensions, rather than sharing that authority and responsibility with the trial court, and subjects such motions for additional time to careful scrutiny. Active management of the caseflow requires the existence and occasional exercise of sanctions against those who attempt to abuse the system.

A successful affirmative case management system depends in large part upon two things: court rules written to give appellate courts authority over all stages of the appellate process, and judges who are willing to exercise strong administrative leadership.

> Even if the best possible set of rules has been promulgated, little may happen if those in charge—the court administrator and the chief judge—do not make clear their commitment to see that the rules are followed. In effect, the chief judge can help diminish concern on the part of other judges and the bar by strong and explicit commitment to proposals aimed at reduction of delay. If caseload management is to be used so that the goal of the prompt and just determination of appeals can be realized, the presiding judge must assume supervisory tasks and the other judges of the court must adhere to the court's procedure.[12]

Any proposed solution to appellate delay emphasizes certain aspects of the appellate process, reflects assumptions made about the sources of court delay, and is subject to criticism of one form or another. Yet, even though ideal solutions are non-existent, some solutions may be preferable to others when placed in the context of a particular court's needs and organization.

---

12. Wasby et al., supra note 5, at 73.

16 Appellate Court Delay

The next chapter documents the extent of delay in the ten sample courts, while subsequent chapters identify the probable sources of delay, and describe how some courts have attempted to minimize if not eliminate delay.

Measuring Processing Time and Delay 3

Total appellate case processing time is defined here as the number of days that elapse between judgment in the initial forum, usually a trial court, and the date the appellate court issues the mandate. Although appellate courts customarily measure case processing time from the filing of the appeal to the release of the opinion, this study uses the more comprehensive interval because it represents the total time litigants are involved in appeals and is probably the standard by which they assess appellate court delay. The use of this interval reflects the presumption that the appellate process is an integrated system whose efficient operation is dependent on the actions of a variety of persons. It emphasizes the important roles played by lower court judges and clerks, attorneys, appellate court judges and their staff, and supreme court judges and their support personnel.

To describe fully appellate processing time and to isolate specific problems, the comprehensive time frame was further divided into components corresponding to steps in the appellate process: Step 1, from judgment to "at issue" (when all materials necessary to decide a case have been filed); Step 2, from at issue to oral argument; Step 3, from oral argument to decision; and Step 4, from decision to mandate. For cases in which arguments were not heard, available data did not permit Steps 2 and 3 to be measured separately. Consequently, decision-making time for these cases is measured from the at issue date to the date the opinion was released.

Although common sense tells one that an average of 383 elapsed days to file appellate materials after lower court judgment, for example, indicates delay, more objective standards for determining how frequently excessive processing times actually occur are necessary. Without objective standards, the question of delay remains one of individual perception, and is thus subject to wide interpretation.

Defining delay, however, is a difficult task. As one group of authorities of the judicial process submitted:

> The term delay often is used loosely. In general, people seem to mean that the courts are taking a long time to dispose of cases. But the standard underlying the judgment—that is, what a long time is—normally is left undefined. It also can vary from place to place or person to person. Some time is necessary for the disposition of

17

any case; the question becomes how much of that time is inappropriate and hence constitutes delay.[1]

The standard for determining delay used in this study is the percentage of cases in each court that exceed the court's own rules for completing steps in an appeal. Although this definition is not perfect, the use of each court's own standards avoids the problem of subjecting some court systems to the biases of others. Each court's processing time is analyzed within the context of its own system with its possibly unique rules. The American Bar Association's Commission on Standards of Judicial Administration has promulgated standards that have also been used in this study.

In recognition that all courts allow time extensions, albeit in varying frequency, the examination of the percentage of cases exceeding courts' standards includes data for actual processing time compared not only with the standards expressed by court rules but also compared with the time allowed therein with hypothetical extensions added.

Total Case Processing Time

Analysis of time-lapse data from each sample court reveals that appellate courts differ substantially in the amount of time required to process cases. As indicated in Table 3-1, the average (mean) elapsed time between lower court judgment and appellate court mandate ranged from 240 days in the Oregon Court of Appeals to 649 days in the Illinois Appellate Court, First District.[2] When time distributions are expressed in quartiles, the level of disparity among the sample courts appears even greater than that revealed through a simple comparison of means. In the Oregon Court of Appeals, 75 percent of all cases were processed in 269 days or less, or much faster than the bulk of cases in any other court. At the other extreme, in Illinois it took 799 days or less to dispose of the same percentage of cases.

The ninetieth and ninety-fifth percentile measure are also provided in Table 3-1 to show the effects of cases that require processing time well in excess of that which is routinely required. Analysis of these two measures indicates that, while absolute total day differences among the sample courts are still large, proportionately they are not so large as the differences apparent when non-extreme cases alone were considered.

Table 3-2 presents each court's time distribution by the percentage

---

[1]. Stephen Wasby, Thomas Marvell, and Alex Aikman, *Volume and Delay in State Appellate Courts: Problems and Responses* (Williamsburg, Va.: National Center for State Courts, 1979), p. 6.

[2]. Complete statistical descriptions of the total time interval and all other time intervals for each court are in Appendix A.

of cases disposed of within a series of six-month intervals. Even though the majority of cases in three courts are completed in a year or less after lower court judgment—90 percent in the Oregon Court of Appeals, 71 percent in the Nebraska Supreme Court, and 67 percent in the Florida Court of Appeal, First District—only about 10 percent of the cases in two other courts are completed within the same time period.

Note that in the Virginia Supreme Court only a small fraction of the caseload is completed in less than a year. These data must be interpreted in light of the court's unique structure. The Virginia court follows a two-phased appellate procedure, the first of which averages 280 days, when all petitions are reviewed on their merits by the Supreme Court. Most are denied further consideration. Using this procedure, the Virginia court is able to dispose of the bulk of its caseload in a relatively short time. Cases reflected in Tables 3-1 and 3-2, however, are only those in which petitions for review *were granted*. Thus, these cases had gone through the entire appellate process. The majority of them (75 percent) were disposed of in less than 18 months.

Most of the sample courts had disposed of all but a very small fraction of their total caseloads within two years after lower court judgment, but two courts deviated substantially from this pattern. Percentage figures from the Illinois Appellate Court, First District, and the Indiana Court of Appeals show that nearly one-third of these courts' cases took more than two years to complete.

Components of Total Case Processing Time

Total case processing time is a summation of time elapsed during different phases or steps in the appellate process. As noted previously, an examination of the relative contribution of each step in each court should help to pinpoint accurately where cases are being delayed. Even though two courts might have similar total case processing time averages, the relative contributions of each step in the process might, nonetheless, differ dramatically. Where the points of delay differ, unique solutions might be required. For example, total case processing for oral argument cases in both the Montana Supreme Court and the Florida Court of Appeal averaged about 400 days. Yet, when component parts of the appellate process are examined, these two courts are very different. In Montana, an average of 242 processing days was required during Step 1, while in Florida only 170 days were required. At Step 2, 143 days, on the average, had elapsed in the Florida court, but only 82 days in Montana. Thus it is likely that these two courts, though having similar total case processing time, are challenged by problems that are isolated in different parts of the appellate process. Consequently, one cannot assume that reforms designed to speed up the process in Florida would necessarily work in Montana.

TABLE 3-1
Total Case Processing Time Distributions in Days:

Court	N Cases	First Quartile (25%) Days
Oregon Court of Appeals	(406)	174
Nebraska Supreme Court	(603)	224
Florida Court of Appeal, First District	(337)	210
Montana Supreme Court	(463)	252
New Jersy Superior Court, Appellate Division	(395)	250
Ohio Court of Appeals, Eighth District	(358)	216
Colorado Court of Appeals	(660)	310
Virginia Supreme Court	(288)	427
Indiana Court of Appeals	(338)	459
Illinois Appellate Court, First District	(311)	468

Lower Court Judgment to Appellate Court Mandate Quartiles and Percentiles

Second Quartile (50%-Median) Days	Third Quartile (75%) Days	Ninetieth Percentile (90%) Days	Ninety-fifth Percentile (95%) Days	Mean Days
210	269	358	463	240
305	378	436	479	301
303	401	518	634	333
355	471	622	722	370
384	487	603	654	379
481	565	615	666	413
418	529	674	761	432
483	549	617	650	484
609	795	990	1,129	641
629	799	999	1,093	649

The quartile and percentile figures indicate the upper limits of the range. Theoretically, for example, cases in the first quartile of Oregon could require from one to 174 days.

TABLE 3-2
Percentage of Total Cases Processed

	Oregon Court of Appeals	Nebraska Supreme Court	Florida Court of Appeal, 1st District	Montana Supreme Court
Number	(406)	(603)	(337)	(463)
Percent 1-6 months	31	16	16	14
Percent 7-12 months	59	55	51	38
Total	90	71	67	52
Percent 13-18 months	7	21	24	33
Total	97	92	91	85
Percent 19-24 months	2.7	7	7	11
Total	99.7	99	98	96
Percent 25+ months	.3	1	2	4
Total	100	100	100	100

The Predecision Phase

Table 3-3 presents the average number of days attributable to the four component steps of the appellate process. The data reveal large differences in case processing time among courts at all stages in the appellate process. Time elapsed during the first phase, Step 1, ranged from a 153-day average in the Oregon Court of Appeals, to a 383-day average in the Illinois Appellate Court, First District. Disparity among the sample courts is even greater during Step 2, from an average of 27 days in the Oregon Court of Appeals to nearly ten times as many, 266 days, in the Ohio Court of Appeals, Eighth District. Only two other courts, the Nebraska and Montana Supreme Courts, had averages of less than 100 days during this second phase.

Information presented in Table 3-4 shows that, even though the sample courts differ only moderately in the amount of time specified by court rules for filing all appellate materials—from 120 to 195 days—they differ dramatically in their performance, as evidenced by the wide range of the percentage of cases exceeding court rules in each

at Six-Month Intervals

New Jersey Superior Court Appellate Division	Ohio Court of Appeals, Eighth District	Colorado Court of Appeals	Virginia Supreme Court	Indiana Court of Appeals	Illinois Appellate Court, 1st District
(395)	(358)	(660)	(288)	(338)	(311)
13	23	9	1	2	3
32	8	29	8	11	7
45	31	38	9	13	10
42	37	51	66	28	29
87	68	89	75	41	39
11	29	5	24	28	27
98	97	94	99	69	66
2	3	6	1	31	34
100	100	100	100	100	100

jurisdiction.[3] A majority of cases were processed within established time limits in only two courts, the Virginia Supreme Court and the Oregon Court of Appeals. Use of this strict definition of delay leads to the conclusion that most cases in most courts were delayed. Such a definition of delay, however, may be unrealistic because of the legitimate need for time extensions in many cases. When one 30-day time extension is added to the interval, the percentage of cases exceeding court rules decreases rather regularly in each sample court, and continues to decrease when two extensions—one for the appellant and one for the appellee, for example—and then three extensions are allowed. It is extremely doubtful, however, that so many cases are so complex that they legitimately require such substantial amounts of time in excess of court filing rules. Even when one allows for an additional 90 days beyond filing standards, two sample courts would still not have received the necessary materials in the majority of their

---

3. Complete delay statistical descriptions for all time intervals for each court are in Appendix B.

TABLE 3-3
Steps in the Appellate Process: Mean Time in

COURT	STEP 1 Lower Court Judgment to at Issue
Oregon Court of Appeals N = 317 Oral Argument No Oral Argument	 153 days Incomplete Data
Nebraska Supreme Court N = 358 Oral Argument No Oral Argument	 206 days Incomplete Data
Florida Court of Appeal, First District N = 123 Oral Argument N = 149 No Oral Argument	 170 days 193 days
Montana Supreme Court N = 337 Oral Argument N = 80 No Oral Argument	 242 days 114 days
New Jersey Superior Court, Appellate Division N = 270 Oral Argument No Oral Argument	 261 days Incomplete Data
Ohio Court of Appeals, Eighth District N = 238 Oral Argument No Oral Argument	 186 days Incomplete Data
Colorado Court of Appeals N = 446 Oral Argument N = 51 No Oral Argument	 224 days 227 days
Virginia Supreme Court N = 226 Oral Argument N = 35 No Oral Argument	 304 days 298 days
Indiana Court of Appeals N = 20 Oral Argument N = 299 No Oral Argument	 285 days 292 days
Illinois Appellate Court, First District N = 137 Oral Argument N = 155 No Oral Argument	 383 days 307 days

Measuring Processing Time and Delay 25

Days, Oral-Argument and Non-Oral-Argument Cases

STEP 2 *At Issue to Oral Argument*	STEP 3 *Oral Argument to Decision*	STEP 4 *Decision to Mandate*	MEAN TOTAL DAYS
27 days	24 days	55 days	259 days
76 days	52 days	28 days	362 days
143 days [Steps 2 & 3, 92 days]	64 days	32 days 27 days	409 days 312 days
82 days [Steps 2 & 3, 115 days]	69 days	22 days 6 days	415 days 235 days
137 days	27 days	Not Applicable	425 days
266 days	58 days	18 days	527 days
106 days [Steps 2 & 3, 141 days]	69 days	81 days 71 days	480 days 439 days
111 days [Steps 2 & 3, 155 days]	60 days	18 days 14 days	493 days 466 days
175 days [Steps 2 & 3, 267 days]	74 days	130 days 78 days	663 days 637 days
149 days [Steps 2 & 3, 189 days]	73 days	122 days 104 days	727 days 600 days

TABLE 3-4
Predecision Case Processing Time

	STEP 1 *Trial Judgment to at Issue*		
Court	Court Rule	% Cases Above Rule	% Cases Above Rule + 90 Days
Oregon Court of Appeals	150 days	38	4
Nebraska Supreme Court	130 days	92	32
Florida Court of Appeal, First District	145 days	53	16
Montana Supreme Court	144 days	68	40
New Jersey Superior Court, Appellate Division	160 days	72	53
Ohio Court of Appeals, Eighth District	120 days	64	25
Colorado Court of Appeals	154 days	66	32
Virginia Supreme Court	79 days*	9	2
Indiana Court of Appeals	195 days	75	41
Illinois Appellate Court, First District	177 days	79	57

*Petition granted to materials
**30 days used for comparison; court rules do not specify time limit
***Petition granted to brief

vs. Court Rules

	STEP 1A Record Received to Appellant Brief			STEP 1B Appellant Brief to Appellee Brief		
Court Rule	% Cases Above Rule	% Cases Above Rule + 60 Days	Court Rule	% Cases Above Rule	% Cases Above Rule + 60 Days
45 days	22	3	30 days	54	2
30 days**	96	43	30 days	65	3
30 days**	42	10	20 days	68	7
30 days	84	39	30 days	75	23
Insufficient Data			30 days	73	27
20 days	65	21	20 days	76	20
40 days	76	29	30 days	66	8
40 days***	23	8	25 days	25	1
30 days	45	13	30 days	67	12
35 days	88	56	35 days	82	40

cases. In both the New Jersey Superior Court, Appellate Division, and the Illinois Appellate Court, First District, over one-half the cases still were not perfected after the maximum time allowed under court rules plus 90 days.

The predecision phase was divided further into additional parts, each nominally the responsibility of different actors in the judicial process. Analysis of these different parts revealed that prompt transcript filing was a serious problem in some of the sample courts. A majority of transcripts were filed within time standards in only four of the seven sample courts from which data were available. In the remaining three, the degree of disparity between standard and actual processing time was substantial: from 68 percent in the New Jersey Superior Court, Appellate Division, to 93 percent in the Nebraska Supreme Court. If one 30-day extension is added, the percentage of cases exceeding the standard decreases somewhat, and continues of course to decrease as two or even three extensions are added to the interval. However, even when three extensions are added, records or transcripts[4] had not been filed in a sizable percentage of cases in three sample courts—New Jersey Superior Court, Appellate Division, 32 percent; Indiana Court of Appeals, 44 percent; and Nebraska Supreme Court, 51 percent.

Transcripts were not the only source of delay during the predecision phase of the appellate process. Table 3-4 shows considerable discrepancy between the standards for filing appellant and appellee briefs and actual filing times. In five of the ten sample courts the majority of opening briefs were not filed within the time limitations specified by standards. Moreover, when two 30-day extensions are added to the rules interval, sizable percentages of appellants' briefs were filed in adherence to standards in only one court (the Virginia Supreme Court). With one 30-day extension, the percentage of cases exceeding the hypothetical interval drops substantially in all the sample courts. Nonetheless, as for other predecision stages, in four courts sizable percentages of answer briefs still had not been filed after two or three 30-day extensions had been added to the court's rules.

Excessive brief preparation time was not the result of preparation of exceptionally long or complex briefs. Analysis of the length of appellant's and appellee's briefs indicates that briefs rarely exceed the court's page limitations in any of the sample courts. Although it is difficult to measure, one indicator of case complexity might be the number of issues raised in an appeal. Analysis of court record data revealed that by the "issue" standard most cases were not complex. The average number of issues ranged from 1.3 per case in the Oregon Court of Appeals to 2.9 per case in the Ohio Court of Appeals, Eighth

---

4. See David C. Steelman, William H. Popp, Samuel D. Conti, et al., *Court Reporting Services in New Jersey* (North Andover, Mass.: National Center for State Courts, Northeastern Regional Office, 1978).

District. Most courts reported averages of just under two issues per case.

During Step 2, the "at issue" to oral argument phase, there were no court rules against which to compare time-lapse distributions. A hypothetical standard of 60 days was established purely for purposes of comparison among the courts. Under this standard only one court, the Oregon Court of Appeals, would have processed the majority of its cases. When an additional 30 days is allowed, two more courts—the Nebraska and Montana supreme courts—would have processed the bulk of their cases. If 90 days is added to the hypothetical 60-day standard (for a total of 150 days), all courts but one would have heard a majority of their cases (see Table 3-5). The Ohio Court of Appeals, Eighth District, with 88 percent of its caseload still awaiting oral argument 150 days after submission, was the exception. The probable source of the Ohio problem will be examined in later sections. Note that this waiting period is not necessarily wasted time: in a few sample courts case materials are reviewed by central staff during this period, while in others materials are submitted to panels and judges for preargument preparation.

The Decision-Making Phase

For Step 3, time elapsed between oral argument and decision, the magnitude of the differences among courts is small when compared with differences apparent during the predecision phases. Processing time fell within the relatively narrow range of 25 days in the Oregon court to 74 days in Indiana.

Even though there were also no rules from the sample courts specifying how soon after argument opinions were to be announced, the American Bar Association standards do provide some guidance.[5] In accordance with these standards, all of the sample courts could be said to decide at least a majority of their cases within the maximum allowable time. If 90 days were added to the ABA standards, six of the sample courts would have decided over 95 percent of their cases. Even so, 16 percent of the Indiana Court of Appeals' cases would still be outstanding.

Disparity between the actual processing times and these standards of performance was even greater for non-oral-argument cases. A majority of non-oral-argument cases were decided within the ABA

---

5. These standards are: "For a court sitting in panels of three judges, the average time for rendering decisions should not exceed 30 days; the maximum time for any case, except one of extraordinary complexity, should not exceed 60 days. For a court sitting in larger panels, the average time should not exceed 60 days; the maximum time, except in cases of extraordinary complexity, should not exceed 90 days." American Bar Association, Commission on Standards of Judicial Administration, *Standards Relating to Appellate Courts* (1977), Standard 3.52(b)(4) and commentary.

TABLE 3-5
Decision Processing Time vs. *Steps 2 Through 4*

	STEP 2 AT ISSUE TO ORAL ARGUMENT	
	% Cases Above Hypothetical 60-day Standard	% Cases Above Rule + 90 Days
Oregon Court of Appeals	7	1
Nebraska Supreme Court	56	8
Florida Court of Appeal, First District	91	39
Montana Supreme Court	65	6
New Jersey Superior Court, Appellate Division	81	37
Ohio Court of Appeals, Eighth District	94	88
Colorado Court of Appeals	90	11
Virginia Supreme Court	71	31
Indiana Court of Appeals	88	44
Illinois Appellate Court, First District	90	47

Measuring Processing Time and Delay 31

Court Rules or ABA Standards

STEP 3 ORAL ARGUMENT TO DECISION		STEPS 2 & 3 NON-ORAL-ARGUMENT CASES AT ISSUE TO DECISION		STEP 4 DECISION TO MANDATE
% Cases Above ABA Average	% Cases Above ABA Maximum	% Cases Above ABA Average	% Cases Above ABA Maximum	% Cases Above Hypothetical 30-Day Standard
9	3	Insufficient Data		97
31	9	18	18	12
49	34	91	57	16
45	20	61	43	10
33	11	58	52	Not Applicable
63	40	Insufficient Data		7
72	45	98	93	56
26	6	93	78	7
69	46	99	92	54
81	49	95	91	92

recommended average in only one of the sample courts, the Nebraska Supreme Court. The levels of disparity between actual times and standards for the other courts ranged from 58 percent in the New Jersey Superior Court, Appellate Division, to nearly all cases, 99 percent, in the Indiana Court of Appeals. As shown in Table 3-5, even when 90 days are added to the ABA maximum standards, sizable percentages of cases in most courts (and in two courts the majority of cases) were still awaiting decision.

Average processing time attributable to the final phase, Step 4, in the nine courts (other than New Jersey) in which this interval exists, ranged from 6 days for non-oral-argument cases in the Montana Supreme Court, to 130 days for oral-argument cases in the Indiana Court of Appeals. Neither the courts nor the ABA had standards specifying how soon after the decision the mandates should be issued and recorded. The postdecision phase is important because it is during this phase that petitions for rehearing or for certiorari are filed and because the issuance of mandate represents the irrevocable close of an appeal for most cases. A hypothetical standard of 30 days was used to help assess excessive processing time attributable to this step of the appellate process. Half of the sample courts had completed this final step for the majority of their cases at the end of 30 days, while the remaining one-half exceeded the 30-day standard in a majority of cases. After 90 days had elapsed, or the standard plus 60 days, all the courts had closed the majority of their cases. Yet, in three courts—the Colorado, Indiana, and Illinois appellate courts—a significant percentage of cases, ranging from 18 to 29 percent, still had not been closed even after 120 days had elapsed between decision and mandate.

General Patterns Among Courts

Even though the processing time averages differed substantially among the sample courts at all stages of the appellate process, there are, nonetheless, general patterns common among the entire sample. As indicated in Figure 3-1, which presents time attributable to each step in the appellate process as a percentage of total time, time elapsed during Step 1, Lower Court Judgment to At Issue, and Step 2, At Issue to Oral Argument, represents about three-fourths of the total life of appeals in these courts. In contrast, Steps 3 and 4, the decision phase, account for a relatively small portion of the case processing time in each court.

That approximately three-fourths of total appellate case processing time occurred before oral argument or judges' consideration strongly suggests that efforts to reduce processing time in many courts will require solutions focusing directly on the predecision phases of the appellate process. In many appellate jurisdictions, control over materials preparation traditionally has not been exercised by the appellate

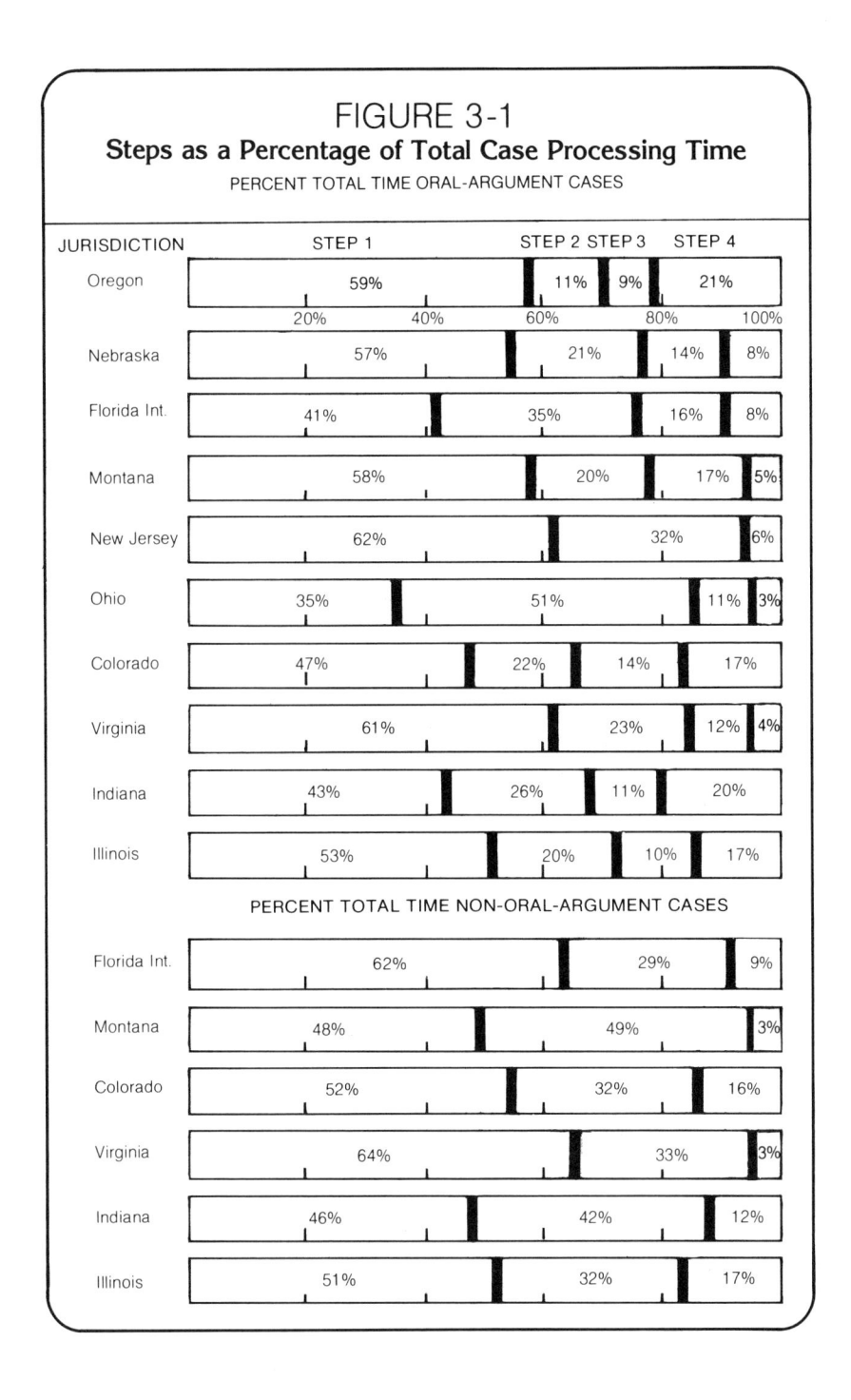

FIGURE 3-1
Steps as a Percentage of Total Case Processing Time
PERCENT TOTAL TIME ORAL-ARGUMENT CASES

JURISDICTION	STEP 1	STEP 2	STEP 3	STEP 4
Oregon	59%	11%	9%	21%
Nebraska	57%	21%	14%	8%
Florida Int.	41%	35%	16%	8%
Montana	58%	20%	17%	5%
New Jersey	62%		32%	6%
Ohio	35%	51%	11%	3%
Colorado	47%	22%	14%	17%
Virginia	61%	23%	12%	4%
Indiana	43%	26%	11%	20%
Illinois	53%	20%	10%	17%

PERCENT TOTAL TIME NON-ORAL-ARGUMENT CASES

JURISDICTION	STEP 1	STEP 2	STEP 3
Florida Int.	62%	29%	9%
Montana	48%	49%	3%
Colorado	52%	32%	16%
Virginia	64%	33%	3%
Indiana	46%	42%	12%
Illinois	51%	32%	17%

Measuring Processing Time and Delay 33

court but rather has been controlled by trial court judges, administrators, and litigants' attorneys. Efficient case processing may require appellate court judges to assume more administrative duties, and hence a broader role than that to which they are accustomed.

Although the primary purpose of this chapter is to describe both the diversity and the commonality among case processing times, it is appropriate to comment briefly on the reasons for the long wait between the filing of materials and oral argument in some courts.

The Step 2 waiting period measurement may be an indirect measure of case backlog. For example, during the period from which data for this study were collected, the Ohio Court of Appeals, Eighth District (the court with the longest average waiting period included in the study) heard by local practice only 78 oral-argument cases per month. At the same time, the court faced a substantial backlog of ready cases. Clearly, it could not significantly reduce its backlog by hearing only 78 cases per month, and cases that could not be heard immediately would have to wait a long period of time for court consideration.

At the other extreme, virtually no case backlog existed in the Oregon Court of Appeals. The Oregon court did not place any restrictions on the number of cases to be heard in any given month.

A long waiting time between at issue and oral argument probably has serious secondary effects on the court system, affecting the materials-preparation time, for example. Many courts with long waiting times between at issue and argument routinely grant time extensions for materials preparation and filing. Courts can justify these practices by recognizing their inability to calendar appeals promptly once they become perfected. If materials were consistently filed within the time limits specified in court rules, the backlogs of ready cases would become even larger.

In addition, it is conceivable that some attorneys, court reporters, and clerks in systems experiencing substantial waits between materials filing and oral argument might be reluctant to prepare and file necessary materials even within the generous time limits allowed by court rules, further coupled with liberal policies for granting time extensions. This reluctance might be due to their perception that even with their court indirectly stretching out the materials-preparation stage by routinely allowing time extensions, cases still would not be heard once all materials were filed, because of substantial case backlogs. Thus, even though processing times attributable to the decision phase of the appellate process, Step 3, are relatively shorter than time attributable to other phases, one should not assume that there are not serious delay problems stemming from the decision phase. In many instances "ready" cases are not being considered promptly but rather are becoming backlogged.

While none of the appellate courts in this study was totally free of delay, the severity of the problem among them differed greatly. In all the courts, at least a few cases exceeded time limitations at some stage of the appellate process. These delays could be viewed as case-specific occurrences in generally efficient court systems. In most courts, however, the time limitations were exceeded routinely at some stages, and in a few courts the majority of cases exceeded time standards at all stages. Delay of the latter type does not reflect mere anomalies within generally efficient court systems, but rather suggests the existence of potentially serious systemic problems. The probable sources of the more systemic types of delay are discussed in the next chapters.

4 Caseload and Delay

The layman might assume that problems of increasing case volume and of appellate court delay are inseparable: that is, that the greater a court's caseload the longer it will take to dispose of cases. Another assumption might be that some types of cases inherently require longer processing times than do others.

Questions Investigated

The Appellate Justice Improvement Project investigated a few of the many questions surrounding these two central issues, using the data collected in the ten sample courts. Specifically, the question of case volume and delay was examined by ascertaining whether or not there were meaningful positive correlations among the ten sample courts between the indicators of case volume and the indicators of case processing time and delay. The two indicators of case volume used in the analysis were the absolute number of filings per year and the number of filings per judge per year in each court. The case processing time and delay measures defined in the preceding chapter were once again used in this portion of the analysis.

Analysis of the relation of case types to case processing time and delay focused on answering two related questions. First, did differences in case type correlate with differences in case processing time within each of the sample courts? Second, if there were meaningful relationships between case types and processing time within a jurisdiction, were the patterns of relationship consistent across jurisdictions, i.e., were the case types that required longer processing time the same from one court to another?

Case-characteristic indicators examined in this analysis[1] were classified under four conceptual categories: the substantive content of appeals,[2] the parties and attorneys involved in appeals,[3] briefs and

---

1. See generally Appendix D.
2. Case subject matter(s), appeal issue(s), number of subject matters, number of issues raised, and the source of appeal.
3. Type of appellant and appellee, total number of appellants and appellees, and type of attorneys.

records,[4] and opinions.[5]

From the standpoint of appellate court reform, the variables examined differ in one very important respect. Some—those that will be labeled *process* variables, e.g., characteristics of briefs, records, and opinions—are more directly under the control of appellate courts than are others, such as the types of parties and attorneys involved in appeals and the substantive content of appeals.

Principal Findings

Volume and Delay

Even though the size of the caseloads varied greatly among the sample courts,[6] volume differences did not correlate with differences in processing time in a direction one would anticipate if the first assumption mentioned earlier were correct. Courts with relatively larger case volumes generally did *not* take longer to process cases than did sample courts with smaller caseloads. More specifically, the analysis revealed that among the sample courts there was at best a very slight tendency for total case processing time and the percentage of cases exceeding court standards (i.e., delay) to increase as absolute case volume increased. Yet there was a moderate to strong tendency for case processing time and delay to *decrease* as the number of filings per judge increased from court to court.[7] In other words, courts with larger caseloads took no longer or only slightly longer to process their cases than did courts with relatively smaller caseloads; moreover, the sample courts with more filings per judge were appreciably faster than courts with relatively fewer cases per judge.[8]

Table 4-1, which presents the raw data used in determining the relationships between caseload per judge and total case processing time (both for all cases filed and for non-settled cases only) illustrates

---

4. Brief lengths, transcript and record lengths, and number and content of motions.
5. Opinion types and lengths.
6. Caseload data were supplied by the same courts. They should be considered approximations of actual workload, and must be interpreted with caution. The practical implications of these limitations for this analysis center on the types of statistical techniques used: rank-order rather than product moment correlations were used as the primary statistical technique. See generally Appendix C for a more complete discussion of the methods used in this portion of the analysis.
7. See Appendix Table C-1.
8. Both Spearman's rank-order correlation coefficients (r_s) and Pearson's product moment correlation coefficients (r) were computed for each variable set. However, only r_s correlation coefficients are reported in this chapter. Correlations using medians rather than means were also computed. Although there were some minor differences in correlation magnitudes when medians rather than means, and r rather than r_s were computed, the direction of relationship and general trends reported in this chapter are consistent regardless of the specific indicators and statistics used. See Appendix C for a more thorough discussion.

TABLE 4-1
Caseload vs. Total Case Processing Time:
Rank Orders, Settlement and Non-Settlement Cases

	Total Processing Time				Filings per Judge
	All Cases		Non-settlement		
	Mean	*Rank*	*Mean*	*Rank*	*Rank*
Oregon Court of Appeals	240	1	265	1	9 (308)
Nebraska Supreme Court	301	2	334	2	4 (88)
Florida Court of Appeal, First District	333	3	362	3	10 (375)
Montana Supreme Court	370	4	402	4	1 (80)
New Jersey Superior Court, Appellate Division	379	5	417	5	6 (229)
Ohio Court of Appeals, Eighth District	413	6	511	7	8 (287)
Colorado Court of Appeals	431	7	469	6	5 (91)
Virginia Supreme Court	484	8	*	*	7 (239)
Indiana Court of Appeals	641	9	642	8	2 (86)
Illinois Appellate Court, First District	649	10	691	9	3 (87)

Time Rank:
1 = least time
10 = most time

Filing Rank:
1 = least filings
10 = most filings

r_s all cases = -.42**
r_s non-settled cases = -.46

*Data not available.
**See Appendix C for discussion of the r_s statistic.

the rank order correlation statistical procedure. The data show negative relationships between total case processing time and case volume among the sample courts, when volume is defined as cases per judge, regardless of whether all cases or only non-settled cases are included in the analysis. Courts with more cases per judge generally were not "slower," but on the contrary were "faster" than courts with fewer cases per judge. For example, the Oregon and Florida courts appear in the processing time order, which ranks the sample courts from fastest to slowest, as the fastest and the third fastest; but these same two courts also have the highest filings per judge.

Focusing on the various steps of the appellate process, Table 4-2 reveals that there was essentially no positive or negative relationship between absolute case volume and time attributable to the predecision phase of the appellate process, but moderate to strong negative relationships between volume per judge and processing time. (Correlations with magnitudes of between .0 and ±.15 indicate near random patterns or no relationship.) When indicators of delay (rather than case processing time) are used, the results suggest a similar pattern of little or no positive or negative relationship between absolute case volume and delay during the predecision stage, but moderate to strong negative relationship between filings per judge and delay. The only difference between these findings and findings presented previously is that when measures of delay rather than processing time are used, the strengths of the negative relationships are greater.[9]

The relationship between absolute case volume and processing time during the second phase of the appellate process (from at issue to oral argument) was weakly positive. As the number of filings among the sample courts increased, Step 2 time increased. Analysis of the relationship between volume and indicators of delay during Step 2 also revealed moderate to strong positive relationships. Again the differences between these findings and those concerning case processing time are ones of magnitude. The positive relationships when delay measures were used were much stronger than when processing time measures were used.

---

9. Even though sample courts with greater average case processing times are also those with higher percentages of cases exceeding their rules, there is the possibility of discrepancy between the two indicators. This is because the sample courts operate under different rules. For example, rules in the Ohio Court of Appeals, Eighth District, specify a total of 120 days for Step 1, submission of all materials, while the Indiana Court of Appeals rules specify a total of 195 days. Consequently, cases in the Indiana court generally could take longer to process than cases in the Ohio court without being considered delayed, in light of the definition of delay used in this study. To provide a more complete picture of the effects of volume, which takes into account differences in rules among the sample courts, this section specifically examines the relationships between volume and delay, i.e., the percentages of cases exceeding each court's own rules, or ABA standards, or hypothetical standards in instances where rules do not exist. With the exception of changing the dependent variable from processing time to percentage of cases exceeding rules, the analytical techniques and the format used here are identical to those used in the previous section.

TABLE 4-2
Volume vs. Processing Time and Delay: Steps in the Appellate Process
Ten Sample Courts

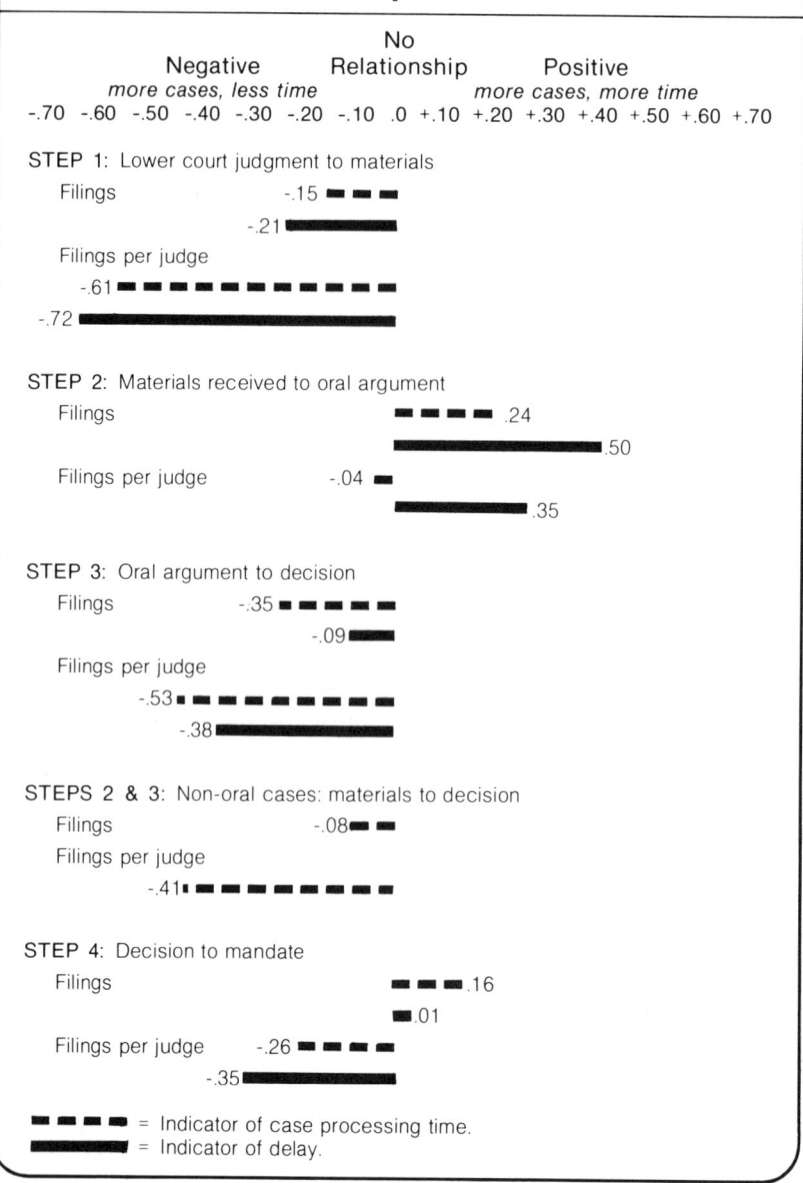

	Negative	No Relationship	Positive
	more cases, less time		*more cases, more time*

-.70 -.60 -.50 -.40 -.30 -.20 -.10 .0 +.10 +.20 +.30 +.40 +.50 +.60 +.70

STEP 1: Lower court judgment to materials
- Filings: -.15 (processing time), -.21 (delay)
- Filings per judge: -.61 (processing time), -.72 (delay)

STEP 2: Materials received to oral argument
- Filings: .24 (processing time), .50 (delay)
- Filings per judge: -.04 (processing time), .35 (delay)

STEP 3: Oral argument to decision
- Filings: -.35 (processing time), -.09 (delay)
- Filings per judge: -.53 (processing time), -.38 (delay)

STEPS 2 & 3: Non-oral cases: materials to decision
- Filings: -.08 (processing time)
- Filings per judge: -.41 (processing time)

STEP 4: Decision to mandate
- Filings: .16 (processing time), .01 (delay)
- Filings per judge: -.26 (processing time), -.35 (delay)

▬ ▬ ▬ ▬ = Indicator of case processing time.
▬▬▬▬▬ = Indicator of delay.

As noted previously, the second step of the appellate process probably reflects case backlog. Clearly, one would anticipate that the absolute number of filings in a court would affect case backlog.[10] Yet the amount of backlog in an appellate court is not a function of case volume alone. Backlog is more likely a function both of volume and of decision-making efficiency; some courts hear and decide cases faster than do others. And at least among the sample courts, those that decided cases relatively faster were not necessarily those with fewer cases to decide. To the contrary, there was a moderately strong tendency for *decision* time (Step 3) to *decrease* as volume increased, regardless of the measures of volume or delay used to compute the correlations.[11] (See Table 4-2, Step 3.)

The relationships between case volume and processing time (specifically, time elapsed during the mid-stages of the appellate process, Steps 2 and 3) are difficult to interpret when non-oral-argument cases are considered separately. Primarily, this is due to the fact that the "waiting" time, Step 2, and the decision time, Step 3, could not be separated into two distinct variables for these cases.[12] Thus, even though the data indicated very weak positive relationships between absolute case volume and time, but very weak negative relationships between volume per judge and time, these results were inconclusive.

Finally, there was virtually no positive or negative relationship between absolute filings and indicators of both postdecision time and delay, but there was a weak to moderate negative relationship between filings per judge and the final step of the appellate process, Step 4.

In general, these findings suggest that the relative importance of case volume as the primary source of appellate court delay has been overemphasized. This does not mean that increasing case volume is unimportant and is something that can be ignored when strategies for court reform are developed. To the contrary, increasing case volume can severely jeopardize the speed with which a court disposes of its caseload. But there are techniques available that can to a great degree compensate for increasing volume, including changes in court procedure, organization, and even structure. Adjustments may be especially necessary in courts experiencing sudden and substantial increases in case volume.

The lack of positive relationships between case volume and delay in the sample courts does not mean that there are not upper limits on the number of cases courts can effectively process, even if compensatory

---

10. Note that this relationship between filings and backlog is a possibility which, as illustrated in the Oregon Court of Appeals, does not necessarily have to occur. (See generally Chapter 5.)
11. Negative relationships were also apparent when only non-settled cases were examined; e.g., volume per judge vs. decision time, Step 3, for non-settled cases only: $r_s = -.30$.
12. The indicator lumps together two potentially distinct events. The two events' interactions may skew the statistical results.

organizational, procedural, and structural adjustments are made. However, the upper limits appear not to have been reached in the courts studied, which have relatively slower case processing time and higher incidences of delay, and it is likely that they have not been reached in other appellate courts across the country. Finally, the findings do not mean that monumental differences in case volume among courts will not result in differences in the seriousness of problems. Clearly one would anticipate that a court with 100 filings per year would face substantially fewer serious problems than would a court with 10,000 filings per year. But volume alone is not the determining or limiting factor for appellate court processing time performance.

Case Types and Delay

Table 4-3 presents data on total case processing time for civil and criminal cases. It reveals that even though there were statistically discernible differences in processing time between civil and criminal cases in five of the ten sample courts, the differences were small and the pattern of the relationship among the courts was inconsistent.[13] Civil cases generally required longer processing time in two of the courts, but in three others the relationship was reversed.

The data also indicate that the magnitude of differences between the civil and criminal categories varied from court to court. Civil cases averaged only about 7 percent more processing time than criminal cases in the Indiana Court of Appeals while in the Colorado Court of Appeals, criminal cases took approximately 29 percent more processing time than civil cases. Finally, the standard deviations accompanying the means for the two categories were generally large in each court, indicating that total case processing times within a single category can vary dramatically from case to case.

Differences in total case processing time *among* the sample courts were not due to differences in relative ratios of civil filings to criminal filings. Where minor differences in processing time between civil and criminal cases did emerge, they were apparently specific to the jurisdictions, occurring in only a few courts rather than in courts in general.

---

13. To determine whether differences among variable category means were statistically discernible, F tests were performed for each nominal level case characteristic variable. If the differences between means were not statistically significant in a sample court, the court was not included in the table. An accompanying .05 significance level value indicates that differences in category means have less than one-twentieth of a chance of being attributable to sampling error. A value of .01 indicates that the possibility of mean differences being attributable to sampling error is less than one in a hundred, while the .001 values signifies a sampling error chance of less than one in a thousand. For detailed discussions of the mathematical properties of F, see Hubert M. Blalock, Jr., *Social Statistics* (New York: McGraw-Hill, 1972) pp. 397-400, and Norman Nie, et al., *Statistical Package for the Social Sciences* (New York: McGraw-Hill, 1975), pp. 259-261.

TABLE 4-3
Total Case Processing Time Variation: Criminal vs. Civil Cases

Jurisdiction	Most Time Mean S.D. N	Least Time Mean S.D. N	Statistical Significance Level
Indiana Court of Appeals	Civil Cases 663 days 274 (174)	Criminal Cases 621 days 267 (163)	.05
Illinois Appellate Court, First District	Criminal Cases 690 days 253 (172)	Civil Cases 598 days 243 (139)	.001
Montana Supreme Court	Criminal Cases 423 days 191 (83)	Civil Cases 358 days 175 (378)	.01
Colorado Court of Appeals	Criminal Cases 517 days 184 (178)	Civil Cases 401 days 189 (478)	.001
Nebraska Supreme Court	Civil Cases 338 days 126 (326)	Criminal Cases 258 days 95 (277)	.05

(Five remaining sample courts: no statistically discernible differences between categories.)

S.D. = Standard Deviation. See Appendix A for explanation.

The same general patterns are apparent when specific criminal and civil case subject matters and issue types are examined.[14] For example, even though processing time did vary by civil subject matter in six of the ten courts, the pattern of variation among courts was inconsistent.[15] None of the six courts displayed the same upper or lower extreme case categories. In fact, in two instances the patterns are contradictory. Cases in the "other administrative law" category had the longest processing time average in the Ohio Court of Appeals, but had the shortest in the Florida District Court of Appeal.

Neither were there meaningful positive or negative relationships

---
14. In the interest of brevity, tables summarizing the relationships between each case processing time interval and each case characteristic are not included in the text, but appear in Appendix D.
15. See Appendix D, Tables D-1 and D-2.

between total case processing time and either the number of subject matters[16] or the number of issues raised as grounds for appeal.[17]

There was little systematic difference between total case processing time and types of appellants and appellees and their counsel. Case processing time averages differed discernibly by appellant/appellee in five of the ten sample courts.[18] Again, where differences between categories did emerge, the patterns of variation are state-specific, not consistent across jurisdictional boundaries. In Ohio, for example, cases involving municipalities as appellants take substantially longer than other cases. This effect does not appear, however, in any other jurisdiction.

The same can be said of minor differences among categories with respect to the types of appellees and their counsel involved in appeals. Differences among categories are not consistent among the sample courts. In the Montana Supreme Court and the Colorado Court of Appeals, cases involving the state as an appellee took slightly longer than cases involving other types of appellees, but in the Nebraska Supreme Court the trend was reversed—cases involving the state as an appellee generally took less processing time.[19]

The relationships between descriptive case characteristic variables and time elapsed during each of the four component phases of the appellate process—materials perfection, waiting, decision, post-decision—were also examined. In the interest of brevity, however, the multitude of tables generated by this analysis revealed the same trends suggested by the examination of total case processing time: little systematic relationship between descriptive case characteristics and time or delay, both within and among sample courts.

These findings support a general conclusion that there is no easily identifiable relationship between the substantive content of cases brought before appellate courts, the types of parties and attorneys involved in cases, and case processing time. There appear to be no case types that inherently require case processing time in excess of that normally required. In those few instances where differences in processing time among categories describing cases did emerge, they were isolated, occurring in only one court, or at most in a few courts, rather than in courts in general. Differences in processing time among cases within any category were usually as great as any differences among categories.

Differences in the mix of cases confronting appellate courts appear then to have little or no effect on the amount of time required to process cases. Virtually any case can theoretically be disposed of within a reasonable time, regardless of the parties involved or the content of the appeal.

---

16. See Appendix D, Table D-3.
17. See Appendix D, Table D-3.
18. See Appendix D, Table D-4.
19. See Appendix D, Tables D-5 and D-6.

Processing Variables and Delay

The analysis did reveal positive relationships both within and among courts between *process* variables, such as extension practices, brief and opinion length, and indicators of case processing time and delay. For example, judges and other court personnel interviewed by project staff indicated that briefs in excess of twenty pages were unnecessary and contributed to unwarranted delay. Data presented in Table 4-4 confirm their suspicions that longer briefs result in longer processing time. Positive relationships between brief length and processing time were apparent in all of the sample courts, though the strength of the relationships varied. But variations in strength of relationships probably are due to differences both in courts' average brief lengths and in rule limitations on brief lengths. Data presented in Table 4-5 illustrate the possible effects of differing court policies.

Specifically, Table 4-5 indicates a moderate to strong tendency for Steps 1 and 3 processing time to increase as brief lengths increase. There are strong positive relationships as well between actual brief lengths and court standards specifying brief page limitations, i.e., the more pages allowed by court standards, the longer the briefs.[20]

Brief length also correlated positively with opinion length. There were moderate to strong positive relationships between brief lengths and majority opinion lengths within all of the sample courts. Perhaps more important, there were also strong relationships between appellant and appellee brief lengths and average opinion lengths *among* the sample courts: courts with longer average brief lengths generally had longer opinions.[21]

Not surprisingly, there were moderate to strong positive correlations between the number of time extensions per case and processing time in all nine sample courts for which data were available.[22] This is, of course, in large part the result of time simply being added to time. The relationship is also due to the fact that extension motions essentially add steps to the appellate process, which in turn add processing time. However, the positive relationship may also indicate that the number of time extensions requested is a function of perceptions of likely delay in latter parts of the appellate process. If an appellate court cannot consistently hear cases as they are ready, judges and other personnel may either implicitly or explicitly encourage attorneys to request extensions, or at the least readily grant them. This is in recognition of the harm that can be engendered in a "hurry up and wait" environment. Table 4-6 illustrates this possibility. Specifically, the data reveal moderate to strong positive relationships

---

20. Brief length specified in court rules vs. actual average: appellant brief length, $r_s=.59$; appellee brief length, $r_s=.78$, and reply brief length, $r_s=.97$.
21. Average appellant brief length vs. average opinion length, $r_s=.65$. Average appellee brief length vs. average opinion length, $r_s=.85$.
22. See Appendix D, Table D-7.

TABLE 4-4
Total Case Processing Time Variation: Amount of Information Provided to Courts

	Length Appellant Brief N	r_s^*	Length Appellee Brief N	r_s	Length Reply Brief N	r_s
Oregon Court of Appeals	(340)	.59	(315)	.59	(34)	.38
Nebraska Supreme Court	(399)	.26	(385)	.37	(99)	-.01
Florida Court of Appeal, First District	(287)	.24	(277)	.28	(126)	.27
Montana Supreme Court	(275)	.17	(364)	.08	(185)	.20
New Jersey Superior Court, Appellate Division			*Insufficient Data*			
Ohio Court of Appeals, Eighth District	(225)	.19	(207)	.19	(43)	-.00
Colorado Court of Appeals	(559)	.24	(530)	.25	(278)	.15
Virginia Supreme Court	(264)	.08	(273)	.09	Too few cases	
Indiana Court of Appeals	(336)	.18	(322)	.19	(151)	.13
Illinois Appellate Court, First District	(238)	.32	(210)	.36	(128)	.25

*See Appendix C for discussion of the r_s statistic.

TABLE 4-5
Variation Among Courts:
Average Brief Length vs. Processing Time and Delay

	Average Appellant Brief Length r_s^*	Average Appellee Brief Length r_s
Step 1: Lower Court Judgment to Materials Filed		
Indicators of processing time	.40	.68
Percent cases above court rule	.73	.77
Percent cases above court rule + 60 days	.46	.68
Step 3: Oral Argument to Decision		
Indicators of processing time	.52	.67
Percent cases above ABA average	.25	.48
Percent cases above ABA maximum	.33	.52
Percent cases above ABA maximum + 60 days	.46	.48

*See Appendix C for discussion of the r_s statistic.

(among the sample courts) between the average number of extensions requested per case and both processing time and delay during the materials-preparation (Step 1) and the decision (Step 3) stages of the appellate process. While it seems reasonable that more extensions would lead to more predecision processing time and delay, it is not clear that extensions lead to more decision time. Attorneys have no reason to request, and courts no reason to grant, time extensions once cases have been submitted and oral arguments heard. Yet the data indicate strong positive relationships between the average number of extensions per case in the sample courts, average decision time, and indicators of delay. It may be that these positive relationships indicate that courts with longer average decision times are simply those that, as a practical matter, are forced to grant more extensions.

TABLE 4-6
Variation Among Courts: Average Number of Extensions vs. Processing Time and Delay

	Average Number of Extensions r_s^*
Step 1: Lower Court Judgment to Materials Filed	
Indicators of processing time	.77
Percent cases above court rule	.51
Percent cases above court rule + 60 days	.70
Step 3: Oral Argument to Decision	
Indicators of processing time	.68
Percent cases above ABA average	.80
Percent cases above ABA maximum	.74
Percent cases above ABA maximum + 30 days	.40

*See Appendix C for discussion of the r_s statistic.

There were weak to moderate positive relationships between the page length of majority opinions and the total case processing time in each of the nine jurisdictions where data were available.[23] As with longer briefs, this suggests that longer opinions might accompany more complex and, in terms of legal substance, more important cases. More complex cases would require more processing time. In addition, longer opinions might simply signal added deliberation and writing time by judges. Table 4-7 indicates that the positive relationships within courts are consistent across the sample courts: courts with longer average opinions generally had longer decision time averages and greater percentages of cases exceeding standards, i.e., more delay, during the decision stage of the appellate process.

Finally, the analysis revealed no substantial difference in total processing time or delay (either within or among courts) among cases

---

23. See Appendix D, Table D-8.

TABLE 4-7
Variation Among Courts: Average Majority Opinion Length vs. Processing Time and Delay

	Average Number of Extensions r_s^*
Step 3: Oral Argument to Decision	
Indicators of processing time	.52
Percent cases above ABA average	.47
Percent cases above ABA maximum	.43
Percent cases above ABA maximum + 30 days	.28

*See Appendix C for discussion of the r_s statistic.

with, or without, dissenting or concurring opinions,[24] despite subjective judicial perception to the contrary in some courts.

The implications of these findings concerning caseload and delay on court reform are generally positive. They suggest that, in terms of processing time, courts are not totally dependent on aspects of the appellate process over which they have little or no direct control: the numbers or types of cases brought before them. Moreover, even though analysis did reveal positive correlation between process case characteristics such as brief and opinion length and delay, it also demonstrated that those aspects of the appellate justice system can be successfully controlled by courts themselves through consistent enforcement of reasonable policies and rules governing extensions and brief and opinion content and length.

---

24. Id.

Structure, Organization and Procedure as Correlates of
5 Case Processing Time:
The Predecision Phase

The analysis presented in the preceding chapter has shown that differences in case volume and case types do not explain the sizable variations in case processing time and measurable delay among the sample courts. These findings suggest that the origins of, and perhaps the solutions to, much appellate court delay lie in court structure and organization. That is, the differences in case processing times among the sample courts are the result of differences in organization and, especially, procedure.

This chapter and the next will examine the relationship between court structure/organization/procedure and case processing time, first at the predecision stages (Steps 1 and 2), then during the decision phase (Steps 3 and 4). Conceptually it was useful to focus the analysis initially on the total processing time interval, then to shift to its four component steps. As a consequence, variations that could directly affect *total* time were presented first, before examinations of features affecting a specific step or steps in the appellate process.

Assessing the Impact of Organization and Procedure

Even though the relationships between court procedure/organization/structure and processing time for each step of the four-phased appellate process are examined separately, it should be kept in mind that any attribute having an identifiable impact on processing time at a specific step will, by definition, affect total case processing time. But in terms of impact, all steps in the appellate process are not equal. The amount of impact any features may have on total processing time will vary dramatically, depending upon the step of the process affected by that feature. As noted previously, time attributable to Step 1 of the appellate process accounts for the largest percentage of total time, nearly 50 percent, when compared to the other three steps, in nine of the ten sample courts. In contrast, time attributable to Step 4, from decision to mandate, accounts for a far smaller share of the case processing time total. Thus, the potential impact on the total processing time of procedural, organizational, and structural features that affect Step 4 would probably be substantially less than the impact of those affecting Step 1.

Total Processing Time

The relationships between two resource-oriented court features—the number of judges per court and the presence or absence of central staff—and total case processing time were examined. (See Table 1-2, page 5, for the number of judges in each of the courts, and Table 5-1 for information on the number and use of central staff.) The analysis shows a positive relationship between the number of judges per court and total case processing time (i.e., those courts with more judges took *longer* to process cases than those with fewer judges), and a negative relationship between the presence of central staff and total time;[1] courts that did not have central staff processed cases *faster* than did courts with central staff.

It is imperative to note that these are not causal relationships. Longer case processing is not caused by more judges or the use of central staff attorneys. The data merely suggest that courts with more judges and with central staff processed cases more slowly than did courts with fewer judges and no central staff for cases filed in 1975 and 1976. Simply adding more judges has been a traditional court response to increased volume and processing time. Consequently, it should not be too surprising that courts with more judges are not necessarily faster courts. The same general conclusion can be offered with regard to central staff. Courts in the sample that are assisted by central staff added these positions during periods of crisis as a reactive measure to radically increased volume.

These findings emphatically do not mean that there are no benefits to be gained by adding judges or by the use of central staff; the scope of this analysis precludes a definitive determination of the efficacy of central staff. Other studies have suggested that the early introduction of central staff or relatively more judges may prevent considerable case processing delay. The findings presented here merely indicate that the presence of central staff or relatively more judges does not guarantee shorter case processing time.

---

1. Number of judges v. total case processing time, $r_s=.56$. Presence or absence of central staff v. total time, tau$=-.38$.

TABLE 5-1
Number and Use of Staff Attorneys

Jurisdiction	Number	Duties
New Jersey Superior Court, Appellate Division	22	Review substantive and procedural motions, prepare research memoranda prior to case assignment to judge.
Virginia Supreme Court	6	At petition stage only: oral presentation to three-judge panel or memorandum preparation re petitions where attorney argues.
Florida District Court of Appeal, First District	3	Case screening for assignment to short argument calendar; preparation of case summaries for cases on "no request" calendar.
Ohio Court of Appeals, Eighth District	0	
Indiana Court of Appeals	0	
Illinois Appellate Court, First District	6	Preparation of draft Rule 23 dispositions.
Nebraska Supreme Court	0	
Montana Supreme Court	0	
Colorado Court of Appeals	3	Accelerated docket: draft opinions; regular docket: preparation of research memorandums.
Oregon Court of Appeals	3	Review substantive motions; review opinions once circulated.

Step 1 Time

The American Bar Association Commission on Standards of Judicial Administration[2] recommends that time elapsed during the predecision phase of the appellate process, from ordering the record to the filing of the last brief, should not exceed 100 days.[3] The ten sample courts specified by rule their time limits for filing case documents, e.g., notice of appeal (NOA), briefs, and record, and some of them were nearly as strict as those recommended by the ABA. The maximum allowed time from trial judgment to submission ranged from 120 days in the Ohio and Oregon courts of appeal to 195 days in the Indiana Court of Appeals. (See Table 5-2.) Note that these were the time periods specified by rule, *not* actual case processing time averages.

Not surprisingly, there is a strong positive relationship between the time allowed by court rules and Step 1 time.[4] When more time is allowed by court rule, case documents are filed over a longer period of time. For example, the Oregon, Florida, and Ohio courts specified by rule relatively shorter filing times. These three courts have the shortest actual filing time averages (153 days in Oregon, 170 days in Florida, and 186 days in Ohio). Moreover, the percentages of cases exceeding court rules in these courts were substantially lower than the percentages for the other sample courts.

At the other end of the spectrum, the Illinois and Indiana courts, which allowed the longest filing time, also had the longest average times at Step 1—385 and 285 days, respectively—and relatively large percentages of cases exceeding court rules (79 and 75 percent respectively).

There was also a positive correlation between filing standards and actual *total* processing time.[5] Courts that took relatively longer during Step 1 did not dispose of cases more rapidly in later steps to "make up" for earlier delays. Rather, as the Step 1 time increased among the sample courts, total case processing time also increased.[6]

Extension Policies

According to the ABA commission, "while a court should be liberal in granting extensions when good cause is shown, it should never grant extensions as a matter of course, permit extensions by stipulation, or delegate to a trial court authority to allow extensions."[7] The wisdom of these recommendations is borne out by this analysis.

There is, of course, a positive relationship between the number of

---

2. American Bar Association Commission on Standards of Judicial Administration, *Appellate Courts* (Chicago: ABA, 1977).
3. ABA, op. cit., p. 86.
4. Time allowed by court rules v. Step 1 time, r_s=.75.
5. Time allowed by court rules v. total time, r_s=.57.
6. Step 1 time with total time, r=.78.
7. ABA, p. 83.

TABLE 5-2
Time Requirements as Specified

Jurisdiction	Trial judgment to Notice of Appeal	Notice of Appeal to Filing of Record
New Jersey Superior Court, Appellate Division	45	30
Virginia Supreme Court	30	60[1]
Florida District Court of Appeal, First District	30	110
Ohio Court of Appeals, Eighth District	30	40
Indiana Court of Appeals	30	90
Illinois Appellate Court, First District	30	63
Nebraska Supreme Court	30	30
Montana Supreme Court	30	40
Colorado Court of Appeals	30	40
Oregon Court of Appeals	30	30

1 From trial judgment to filing record.
2 From trial judgment to filing brief, petition stage.
3 From petition granted to filing brief, appeal stage.
4 Petition stage.
5 Appeal stage.

time extensions per case and Step 1 time (and consequently total time): when more extensions are requested and granted, processing time increases.[8] This direct effect is to be anticipated because, by definition, time is being added to time. To illustrate: Illinois, with the most average time extensions (3.53/case) had the longest Step 1 time average (383 days) and the longest total time average (649 days). Oregon, with the fewest average extensions (.81/case) had the shortest Step 1 time average (153 days) and the shortest total time average (240

---

8. Average number of extensions per case v. Step 1 time, r_s=.78.

by Court Rules — Days

Filing of Record to Appellant's Brief	Appellant's Brief to Appellee's Brief	Appellee's Brief to Reply Brief	Total Judgment to Submission
45	30	10	160
90[2]	14 civ/21 crim[4]	14[6]	104 civ/111 crim[7]
40[3]	25[5]		79[8]
70 civ/80 crim[9]	20	20	140 civ/150 crim
20	20	10	120
30	30	15	195
35	35	14	177
60	30	10	160
30	30	14	144
40	30	14	154
60 civ/30 crim	30	30 (civ only)	180 civ/120 crim

6 Appeal stage only.
7 Petition stage.
8 Petition granted to submission.
9 Notice of appeal to appellant's brief.

days).

Most of the sample courts did not follow a single courtwide policy with regard to extensions, but a common pattern does emerge. With the exception of Virginia,[9] the first request for an extension, usually for 30 days, was granted routinely. Beyond this, extension policies differed dramatically, not only from one court to the next, but from one panel to the next, and even from one judge to another on the same

---

9. In the Virginia Supreme Court, at the petition stage, extensions of time are rarely granted.

court. Most of the judges interviewed said that in their opinion no more than three extensions should ever be granted to file any single document. Yet in several courts the data show that a fourth or fifth extension to file an opening brief, for example, was frequently granted.

But the issues concerning extensions are more complex than the number requested or granted.[10] The analysis demonstrates that where the authority to grant extensions is vested in more than one court, Step 1 time increases.[11] The situation appears especially acute when extensions to file the same document, e.g., records, can be secured first from a trial court, then the appellate court.[12]

As indicated in Table 5-3, contrary to the ABA Commission's recommendation, procedures in several of the states allowed trial courts to grant extensions for filing the notice of appeal (NOA), record, and transcript. There were limits on the length of extensions trial courts could grant: extensions beyond this maximum required review by, and approval of, the appellate court. Appellate judges interviewed by the project staff said that trial judges rarely refused extension requests. All other extensions, e.g., for brief filing, were under the control of appellate courts in each sample jurisdiction.

The procedure in the Illinois appellate system illustrates the effect of a split of authority. Extensions for a single document could be granted first by a trial court and then by the appellate court. Moreover, authority for granting extensions was further fragmented among the five presiding judges of the court, who were responsible for the disposition of such motions in cases assigned to their divisions. Given the separation of the courts, and the autonomy of the appellate court's divisions, implementation of a courtwide policy on extension motions has been impossible.

Table 5-4 compares the distribution of extension requests for the Illinois, Oregon, and Nebraska courts. The Oregon court was selected because it was both the fastest court in terms of total case processing time and the court with the lowest extension-request rate. The Nebraska court represented the average court in terms of both. The Illinois court, as previously mentioned, had the longest average total case processing time as well as the most extensions. The distributions presented in Table 5-4 clearly illustrate a strong tendency for multiple requests for extensions per case in Illinois, as compared with fewer multiple requests in Oregon and Nebraska. For example, 68 percent of all the cases in the Illinois sample included more than one extension request, while only 21 percent of the Oregon cases and 38 percent of the Nebraska cases had more than one request. Moreover, 52 percent of the Illinois cases had more than two extension requests, compared with only 9 percent in Oregon and 14 percent in Nebraska.

---

10. See generally Wasby et al., pp. 71-73.
11. Appellate or trial court authority with Step 1 time, tau=.47.
12. Mixed authority or delineated authority with Step 1 time, tau=.67.

TABLE 5-3
Courts That Grant Extensions

Jurisdiction	To File Notice of Appeal	To File Record/ Transcript	To File Briefs
New Jersey Superior Court, Appellate Division	Appellate Court	Appellate Court	Appellate Court
Virginia Supreme Court	Not Applicable	Not Applicable	Appellate Court
Florida District Court of Appeal, First District	Not Applicable	Trial Court	Appellate Court
Ohio Court of Appeals, Eighth District	Not Applicable	Trial Court (30 days) Appellate Court	Appellate Court
Indiana Court of Appeals	Not Applicable	Appellate Court	Appellate Court
Illinois Appellate Court, First District	Appellate Court (30 days)	Trial Court (42 days) Appellate Court	Appellate Court
Nebraska Supreme Court	Trial Court (30 days)	Appellate Court	Appellate Court
Montana Supreme Court	Trial Court (30 days)	Trial Court	Appellate Court
Colorado Court of Appeals	Trial Court (30 days)	Trial Court (50 days) Appellate Court	Appellate Court
Oregon Court of Appeals	Not Applicable	Appellate Court	Appellate Court

58   *Appellate Court Delay*

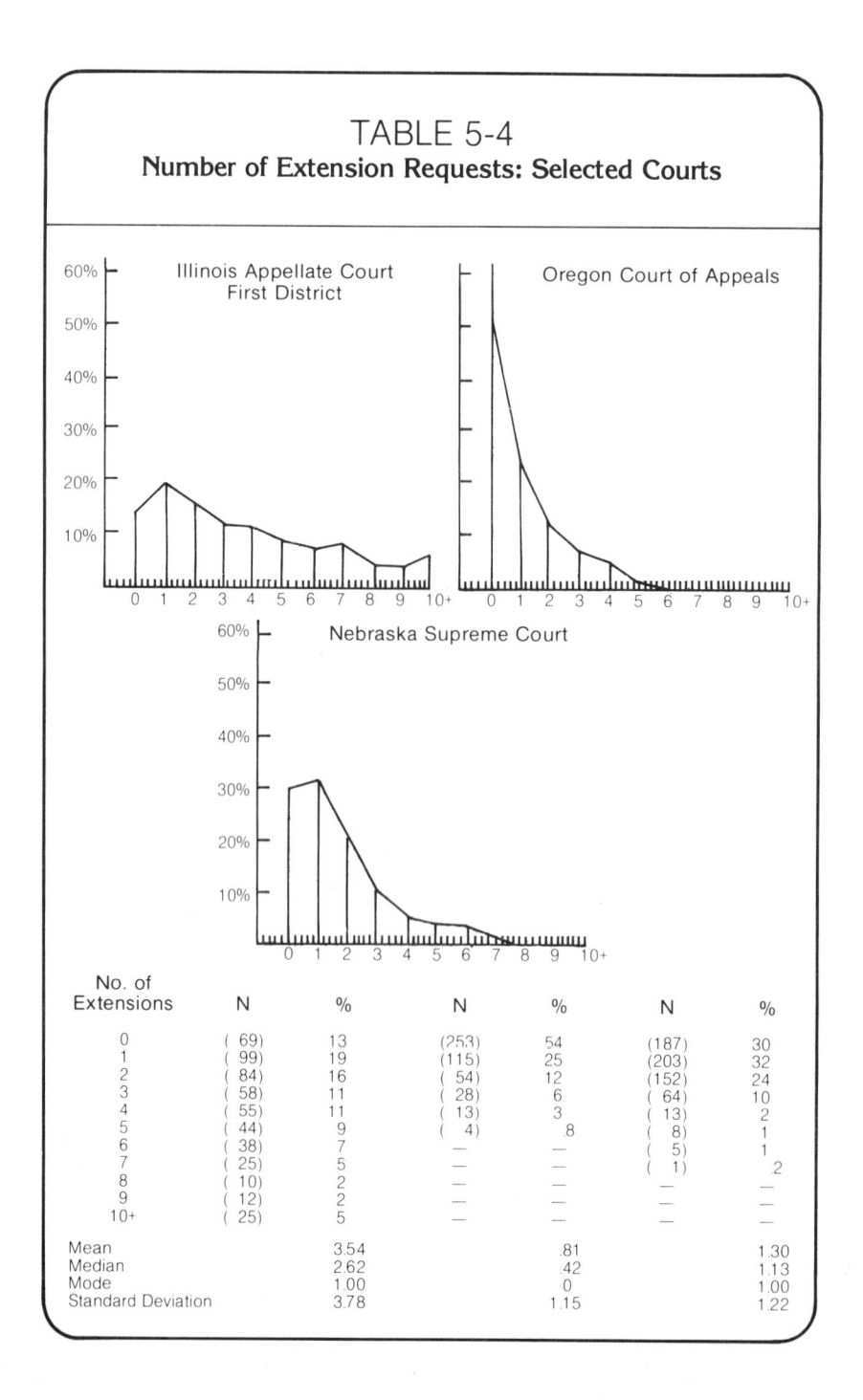

TABLE 5-4
Number of Extension Requests: Selected Courts

Illinois Appellate Court First District

Oregon Court of Appeals

Nebraska Supreme Court

No. of Extensions	N	%	N	%	N	%
0	(69)	13	(253)	54	(187)	30
1	(99)	19	(115)	25	(203)	32
2	(84)	16	(54)	12	(152)	24
3	(58)	11	(28)	6	(64)	10
4	(55)	11	(13)	3	(13)	2
5	(44)	9	(4)	.8	(8)	1
6	(38)	7	—	—	(5)	1
7	(25)	5	—	—	(1)	.2
8	(10)	2	—	—	—	—
9	(12)	2	—	—	—	—
10+	(25)	5	—	—	—	—
Mean		3.54		.81		1.30
Median		2.62		.42		1.13
Mode		1.00		0		1.00
Standard Deviation		3.78		1.15		1.22

Management of cases after filing presents a problem for many appellate courts. Effective control is dependent on many factors, including timing (i.e., the point at which the appellate court, as opposed to the trial court, exercises jurisdiction over appeals), sophistication of the case tracking system, clerical resources, and availability and use of sanctions.

The analysis shows clearly that the use of modern management techniques correlates positively with shorter Step 1 time. Those courts that recognized, by the investment of court resources, the importance of these early stages in the appellate process did move cases more rapidly here.

The difficulties of effective caseload control are compounded in some courts because so many of the early steps for initiating and docketing appeals occur in trial courts. In most jurisdictions the NOA is filed in the trial rather than the appellate court. Typically, records on appeal, including the transcripts, are designated, prepared, often reviewed by, and initially filed in trial courts. Trial court clerks are then usually responsible for forwarding records to appellate courts. In several of the jurisdictions examined, including Florida and Nebraska, records remained on file in the trial courts until after the attorneys had prepared briefs.

There have been a few efforts to introduce early control of the caseload by the appellate court. In New Jersey the original of the notice of appeal (NOA) is filed with the appellate court, and a copy is filed with the court from which the appeal is taken. In Oregon, trial courts are required to forward copies of the NOA to the Court of Appeals upon receipt; in Colorado, attorneys are required to file a designation of parties with the appellate court. These practices, however, are not widespread.

The sophistication of mechanisms to monitor caseload progress also varies dramatically among courts.[13] In Oregon, a computerized case control system was in operation at the time of the sample; due dates for filing all appeal documents were set automatically by computer upon receipt of the NOA. The computer then operated as a daily tickler system, notifying court personnel when materials were overdue. At the other extreme, the Montana Supreme Court only recently had developed a basic manual tickler system. There, when preparing the monthly docket for the all-court conference, the clerk would draw the judges' attention to cases that were overdue. Usually, however, delinquent cases could not be identified until after they had already fallen 30 to 60 days out of sequence. In Nebraska, the court clerk used a similar system, relying upon preparation of the monthly statistical report to identify late cases.

---

13. William H. Popp and Lorraine Moore Adams, *A Study of the New Jersey Appellate Division's Clerk's Office* (North Andover, Mass.: National Center for State Courts, 1979) pp. 151-66.

One reason for these inconsistencies in monitoring practices among appellate courts may be that judges and administrators disagree as to when appeals should be under the control of their courts instead of under trial courts. When interviewed, some judges were obviously uncomfortable with the idea of exercising early caseload control, and preferred to wait until after all traditional trial court activities, including the preparation of transcripts and records, were completed. Others felt that appellate courts should exercise control over all aspects of the appellate process, beginning from the date a NOA is filed. This difference in judicial attitude may be crucial: where the appellate judges are hesitant to assert control over the case on appeal during the early stages, or where they underemphasize the importance of this part of the process, it is unlikely that sufficient resources will be allocated at that point. Longer Step 1 time, and consequently longer overall processing time, may be the result.

In some courts, effective management of the caseload is hindered as well by an insufficient number of clerical personnel, who may also be working in a crowded facility with outdated equipment. Increasing Step 1 time is a virtually inevitable consequence. The situations of the New Jersey and Indiana courts, where Step 1 time averaged 261 and 285 days respectively, are illustrative: these courts simply did not have adequate clerical means to process cases rapidly.[14]

Finally, if appellate courts are unable or unwilling to impose sanctions against those who chronically abuse the appellate process, filing standards will not serve the purpose of regulating participant performance. Without sanctions, filing standards may be little more than "New Year's resolutions"—carelessly adopted, then ignored because impractical.

The disparity in judicial attitudes towards caseload control, mentioned earlier, is also reflected by differences in court sanction policies. Courts vigorously disagree as to when and how sanctions should be imposed. For example, the prompt preparation of trial transcripts by a few court reporters was at one time a serious problem in Oregon. The Court of Appeals responded by issuing contempt orders and demanding the withdrawal of tardy reporters from trial courtrooms until they had completed delinquent transcripts.

Many appellate courts, at least theoretically, could impose similar sanctions. But the need to preserve cordial relations with trial court personnel may preclude the exercise of this option. It is doubtful that trial court judges would be so sympathetic to the problems of appellate courts that they would favor the imposition of sanctions that could disrupt their own dockets. Moreover, in some jurisdictions (e.g., Indiana, at the time of this writing) court reporters are county employees with considerable political clout. Appellate judges may be powerless to resolve the continuing problem of tardy transcripts in

---

14. Ibid.

like jurisdictions.

But for the most part, the analysis to this point has demonstrated that the procedures or policies that have an impact on processing time during Step 1 are within the control of appellate courts. Court rules can be altered and enforced. Uniform, strict, extension policies can be implemented by appellate courts themselves. Effective case monitoring mechanisms are available. Moreover, adequate clerical staff, space, and equipment can be acquired within the confines of legislative appropriations. What is required first is a recognition by courts of the critical importance of, and a commitment to, effective management during the initial phase of the appellate process.

Step 2 Time

The amount of time that elapsed from the perfection of an appeal to the date of oral argument ranged from a low of 27 average days in Oregon to a high of 266 days in Ohio, or from 11 to 51 percent (averaging about 26 percent) of total time.

This analysis examined, among others, the following features for potential impact on Step 2 time: oral argument scheduling practices, especially as affected by geography; use of central staff; preargument settlement conferences; and assignment procedures.

Argument-Scheduling Practices

The single factor most directly affecting Step 2 time is the presence of artificial limitations on the number of arguments heard per court session. In courts where volume is rising rapidly, Step 2 time will increase when the number of judges hearing cases is fixed (as in most courts) and the number of arguments scheduled is also predetermined.

All of the sample courts limited the number of oral argument days each month. Most also set a maximum on the number of oral arguments in a given period (day or week). (See Table 5-5.) In the Montana Supreme Court the justices heard no more than four arguments per day, one week per month. In Ohio, the judges sat for arguments three weeks per month, with each of three panels hearing thirty-six arguments during that month. (Ohio has recently instituted this schedule of 108 cases per month as a response to lengthening Step 2 time. Before 1980, the court heard 78 cases per month, which, because of rising case volume, resulted in a sizable backlog of ready cases and the longest average processing time—266 days—at this step of any of the sample courts.)

The Oregon Court of Appeals, however, scheduled all ready cases for the next calendar period. In September 1978, the then 10-judge Oregon Court had 167 cases on its oral argument calendar and was able to dispose of all those cases within the month. The Oregon example is not cited to suggest that a monthly calendar of 167 cases is necessarily the best standard. Oregon merely illustrates that hearing and deciding more cases than courts traditionally have decided is not impossible, and that many appellate courts have likely not reached their limits. Artificial, unexamined limits on the number of cases a court will hear may simply preclude the court from reaching its maximum desirable case processing potential.

Table 5-5 includes information on whether oral argument was scheduled automatically or had to be requested by counsel. Generally, courts with an automatic scheduling procedure had shorter Step 2 time than did courts where argument had to be requested.[15] It is conceivable that request systems are generally slower because they introduce an additional decision point into the appellate process and present another issue that must be considered by the court. This may require more time than a simple bookkeeping entry in the clerk's office.

Argument scheduling becomes more complex, with a resultant increase in Step 2 time, when judges must travel to other sites to hear and decide cases. Usually a court will wait for a sufficient number of cases to be perfected to fill a calendar before scheduling argument. Consequently, some cases may wait a substantial period of time before oral argument is heard.

This problem appeared to be especially serious in the Florida court, where the judges traveled to each circuit headquartered within the district to hear cases. Some of these locations were visited only a few times a year. Step 2 time was comparatively long in this court, both in terms of absolute days (143) and as a percentage of total time (35 percent).

In New Jersey, where the Appellate Division judges were scattered across the state, with panels coming together only to hear arguments or decide cases submitted on the briefs, the court was hesitant to schedule cases before an entire day of argument could be set. In such an instance, even non-argument cases may be delayed until a conference can be set.

Courts that employ central staff attorneys usually require that their work be done during this second stage (either screening cases, preparing research memoranda, or drafting disposition orders). The presence of central staff might be expected to slow down processing at Step 2 but shorten overall disposition time by reducing processing time at Steps 3 and 4. The data, however, do not support this speculation. As pointed out at the start of this chapter, courts with central staff had longer total case processing time averages than did courts without central staff. Moreover, at Step 2, there was essentially no positive or negative relationship between the presence or absence of central staff and processing time.[16]

One possible explanation for this result is that the functions

---

15. Automatic/no automatic oral argument v. Step 2 time, tau=.48.
16. Presence or absence of central staff v. Step 2 time, tau=-.12.

performed by central staff were not uniform in the six of the ten sample courts that were assisted by such counsel. (See Table 5-1, p. 52.) Staff attorneys in the New Jersey and Colorado courts prepared detailed research memoranda prior to case assignment; these were sent to the judges with accompanying case files, records, transcripts, and briefs. In Colorado, one staff attorney worked exclusively on accelerated docket cases; in New Jersey, four staff attorneys were assigned to the clerk's office, where they assisted in disposing of motions.

Two of the sample courts, the Florida Court of Appeal, First District, and the Illinois Appellate Court, used central staff to screen cases, reviewing them for possible alternative disposition, usually summary disposition. In Florida, staff attorneys screened incoming appeals for assignment to a short-argument calendar. In Illinois, the staff director reviewed incoming appeals for possible assignment to a central staff attorney for summary disposition under Court Rule 23.[17]

In the Virginia Supreme Court, staff attorneys participated only in the petition stage of the appeal process. In cases where counsel did not argue the merits of a petition, staff attorneys made oral presentations to a three-judge panel; where counsel did argue, staff attorneys sometimes prepared research memoranda for judges.

In Oregon, one staff attorney worked solely on motions dispositions, while two others wrote and reviewed opinions after oral argument. These two staff attorneys were unique among the sample courts, because they had responsibilities in the post-argument, rather than the predecision, phase of the appellate process.

The courts also differed in the types of attorneys used for central staff. Illinois and Florida preferred younger attorneys, closer in background to law clerks. Oregon and Colorado have chosen to use more experienced career-path attorneys. Virginia and New Jersey used a mix of both younger attorneys and experienced supervising attorneys, or a chief staff attorney.

Those courts that use a preargument settlement conference technique may schedule this during Step 1 or 2. The analysis consequently considered potential impact at both steps. Unfortunately, since only two of the sample courts used this technique during the period studied, no statistical conclusions concerning its effect on processing time can be drawn.[18] Nevertheless, an examination of the technique's use in those and other courts does allow the following observations.

---

17. Under R. 23 of the Illinois Supreme Court Rules, a case may be disposed of by order where an opinion would have no precedential value, where no substantial question is presented, or where the court is without jurisdiction. It is common practice for the central staff to draft such orders for judicial review.
18. Another part of the Appellate Justice Improvement Project has set up controlled experiments, three of them dealing with preargument conferences. The results of these programs may answer some of these questions.

TABLE 5-5

Jurisdiction	Automatic or Requested
New Jersey Superior Court, Appellate Division	Requested
Virginia Supreme Court	Automatic[1]
Florida District Court of Appeal, First District	Requested
Ohio Court of Appeals, Eighth District	Automatic
Indiana Court of Appeals	Requested[5]
Illinois Appellate Court, First District	Requested
Nebraska Supreme Court	Automatic
Montana Supreme Court	Automatic
Colorado Court of Appeals	Automatic[7]
Oregon Court of Appeals	Automatic

1 Judges may request waiver of oral argument at petition stage in criminal case.
2 Appellant allowed fifteen minutes at petition stage; appellee doesn't argue.
3 Both sides allowed thirty minutes at appeal granted stage.
4 Prior to 1979, attorneys allowed thirty minutes per side.

Scheduling of Oral Argument

Minutes Per Side	Number of Arguments per Session
30	One argument day per week per panel; no daily limit on number of arguments.
15[2]/30[3]	One week of argument every seven weeks, approximately 26 cases that week.
20	Full calendar: six days per month, six cases per day, summary calendar: two days per month, twelve cases per day.
15[4]	Three argument weeks per month, 108 cases per month.
30	—
30	Each division assigned one day per week; four to five arguments per day.
30	Six oral argument days per month; in divisions, 55 arguments per month; en banc, 36.
40/30[6]	One week per month; four per day.
30/15[8]	Approximately 18 per month per division.
30	Approximately eight days per month; all ready cases heard.

5 Arguments almost never heard.
6 Appellants allowed forty minutes; appellee allowed thirty minutes.
7 Regular docket — thirty minutes; accelerated docket — fifteen minutes.
8 Regular docket — thirty minutes; accelerated docket — fifteen minutes.

66   *Appellate Court Delay*

As discussed in Chapter 2, there are a number of reasons why such a program may lengthen time at Steps 1 and 2, and consequently increase total time. First, a conference may add an additional step to the appellate process. (The data do show that processing time increased as the number of steps in that process increased. This phenomenon will be examined in greater detail in Chapter 6.) Second, many courts that hold settlement conferences require that preparation of some documents (e.g., transcript and briefs) be suspended until after the conference is held. If the conference is unsuccessful, and a settlement is not reached, the record and briefs still must be prepared, and hence disposition of the appeal will be delayed until they are ready. Third, where there are scheduling difficulties, the conference itself may be postponed for a considerable time and such postponement may result in postponement of subsequent steps.

The advantage of a preargument settlement procedure is that it may encourage early settlement of cases that either may never have settled or may have settled much later in the process, after litigants had incurred considerable expense.[19] Earlier disposition will decrease the amount of time and attention that both judges and administrative personnel (and central staff, if used) must devote to the consideration and resolution of appeals. This advantage, however, can be realized only if the case does indeed settle. If it does not, total case processing time may increase unless the conference procedure is designed carefully to avoid these pitfalls.

Some court personnel interviewed by the project staff indicated that they thought the conference procedure did slow down processing time. In Colorado, for example, the Court of Appeals decided to exempt cases assigned to the accelerated docket from the conference procedure, anticipating that the procedure might slow down the disposition of these cases. In the Ohio Court of Appeals, Eighth District, though there was concern about the length of processing time for settlement conference cases, the program was discontinued for other reasons.

Assignment Procedures

Ideally, case assignment methods should help assure that appellate court workloads are generally balanced among judges, and among panels in multi-panel courts. In addition, case assignment methods should be such that they "...avoid any suspicion of manipulation that could affect decisions."[20] The American Bar Association Commission on Standards maintains that "...a random assignment procedure accomplishes both objectives."[21] Yet many appellate courts, including some of the courts examined, do not share the ABA's confidence in random assignment procedures.

---

19. Ch. 2, n. 7.
20. ABA, op. cit., p. 91.
21. Ibid.

Only one sample court, the Illinois Appellate Court, First District, assigned cases to divisions using a strictly "blind" procedure: upon filing, cases were assigned to divisions using a computer-generated random number sequence. Usually, appellate courts assigned cases using techniques similar to that used in the New Jersey Superior Court, Appellate Division. By simple sequential rotation, cases were assigned to panels and then to individual judges. The pattern of assignment, however, took into account individual judge backlog, work habits, disqualifications, and sometimes case mix.

Achieving random case assignment may be further frustrated by jurisdictional peculiarities. In the Indiana Court of Appeals, the geographic origin of cases determined their district assignment, but case assignments to judges within a district were by strict rotation.

Many appellate courts do not assign cases using "blind" rotation systems. For example, the Chief Judge in Oregaon personally assigned cases to panels, and ultimately to an individual judge. The Chief Judge in Colorado sent all cases to panels without the benefit of a rotation method. The Chief Justice in Nebraska initially determined whether a case would be heard en banc or in a panel.

But the key aspect in preargument assignment of cases to panels or to individual judges is flexibility of that assignment. Step 2 processing time is affected adversely by the inflexible assignment of cases to parts of a court. When a court is divided into panels or divisions, to which cases are assigned with no provision for reassignment, processing time increases. The lack of transfer procedures to help balance caseloads (where, for example, prolonged illness or disability has resulted in a backlog in one part of the court) can lead to inordinate delay in hearing cases as they become perfected. Clearly, oral arguments may be postponed. Emergency reassignment of cases, in the absence of a formal, well-recognized procedure, is not without problems: appeals can become identified as "someone else's work," and there may be resentment among the other judges if such reassignment is attempted.

6 Case Processing Time During the Decision Phase

In recent years much attention has focused on the question of how appellate courts should be organized to improve their decision-making performance. There is, however, little consensus on how this is to be accomplished. This lack of consensus is illustrated by the great variety of internal organizations and procedures followed during the decision phase, Steps 3 and 4.

Organization of Decision-Making Authority

The American Bar Association Commission on Standards of Judicial Administration stresses that the "primary responsibility of a supreme court is that of developing and maintaining consistency in the law to be applied in subordinate courts in the system."[1] To achieve this, the ABA recommends that "the supreme court should sit en banc...all members of the court should participate in the decision of each case."[2] In contrast, the ABA does not specify so clearly the role of intermediate appellate courts in the process. It seems apparent, however, that these courts should be responsible for reviewing all cases brought into the appellate process. To do this effectively, intermediate appellate courts should "...sit in panels of at least three judges, with all judges participating in the consideration of each case before the panel of which they are members."[3] In addition, to avoid problems of "...decisional inconsistency and discrepancy in procedural policies and practices..."[4] panel membership should be changed periodically, and courts that sit in more than one panel should have "...internal procedures for maintaining decisional consistency."[5]

---

1. American Bar Association Commission on Standards of Judicial Administration, *Standards Relating to Appellate Courts* (Chicago: American Bar Association, 1977).
2. Ibid., p. 7.
3. Ibid.
4. Ibid., p. 10.
5. Ibid., p. 7.

68

Panel Structure

Even though nine of the ten sample courts were subdivided into panels of from three to five judges, philosophies and policies regarding panel rotation varied greatly among them. At one extreme, judges in the Indiana and Oregon courts sit in permanent panels. This was a result of statutory requirement in Indiana: each panel was assigned to a geographically defined jurisdiction, despite the fact that all the panels sat in Indianapolis. In Oregon, non-rotation was simply a matter of court preference. At the other extreme, panel membership was rotated weekly in the Ohio Court of Appeals, Eighth District; in the Florida District Court of Appeal, First District, panels rotated monthly. In the Colorado Court of Appeals, panels rotated once every four months, and in the New Jersey Superior Court, Appellate Division, annually.

There were also other noteworthy policy variations. Three district judges might be temporarily assigned to the Nebraska Supreme Court to enable it to sit in two five-judge panels, which rotated monthly. The Illinois Appellate Court, First District, was divided into five autonomous four-judge divisions. While judges in any one division rotated weekly into three-judge panels, there was no rotation across divisional lines. Judges were assigned to a division by the Supreme Court usually on a permanent basis, though some reassignments had occurred, usually when new judges took office.

Interviews with judges from each sample court provided little insight into what was the "best" technique for organizing judge power: judges uniformly supported the policies of their court. In courts where panels rotated, judges indicated that periodic rotation encouraged judge collegiality because it assured all members contact with each other. In courts where panels did not rotate, judges indicated that non-rotation results in a more efficient system, because it enabled them to learn each other's work habits.

Panel Conflicts

When courts are divided into panels, it is inevitable that conflicts between panels will occur. Most of the sample courts had developed mechanisms to resolve or minimize the effects of conflicts between and among panels, though the sophistication of the techniques varied greatly. One popular technique was to provide for consideration of all opinions in a weekly all-court conference. In Nebraska, the court could rehear cases en banc if necessary to resolve conflicts. Similarly, decisions could be reversed by the entire court at court conferences in the Oregon Court of Appeals.

In the Florida First District Court of Appeal, pending panel decisions that modified prior decisions would be brought to the attention of the court's other judges, and a court conference would be held to resolve the conflict, if necessary. In the Virginia Supreme Court, motions for rehearing were circulated among all judges upon denial of petitions.

There were no mechanisms to resolve conflicts among divisions in either the Illinois Appellate Court, First District, or the Indiana Court of Appeals. Even though the Illinois Supreme Court was required to resolve conflicts among districts, it was not required to resolve conflicts between divisions in a single district. In Indiana, the districts circulated opinions to the whole court before announcement of decisions. This was done primarily as a matter of courtesy, not as a technique to resolve conflicts. The Indiana Supreme Court was not required to settle disputes between districts.

The Ohio and New Jersey courts had developed informal mechanisms to identify conflicts among panels. In Ohio, the court had established an index of unpublished opinions, to assist the judges in determining whether a particular issue had been decided previously by another panel of the court. The judges were not required, however, to follow previous unpublished decisions. In New Jersey, one responsibility of the staff attorney director was to apprise judges of potential conflicts.[6]

Analysis

A number of factors were analyzed with regard to decision time and the use of panels. First, did a court use panels? If so, how many judges sat on each panel? Did they rotate? How often? Finally, was there a mechanism for resolving disputes between the panels?

The results indicated that the simple existence of panels had no positive or negative effect on processing time.[7] Nor did the size of the panel have a strong impact on Step 3, though there was a tendency for larger decision units to dispose of cases faster. Moreover, the number of panels in a particular court did not appear to relate positively or negatively to processing time.[8]

The analysis indicates, however, that decision time is generally shorter in courts that sit in panels and rotate their membership than it is in courts that sit in permanent panels.[9] In addition, the presence of a conflict-resolution mechanism—an all-court conference, provision for en banc decisions, or even frequent rotation—relates positively to shorter disposition time during Step 3. For example, in Indiana and Illinois, which had no such mechanisms, decision times were longer (73 and 74 days, respectively, on the average) than they were in the other sample courts.

---

6. Panels or no panels with Step 3 time, tau=.03. Non-oral-argument cases: panels or no panels with Steps 2+3 time, tau=.17.

7. Number of panels with Step 3 time, r=−.05. Non-oral-argument cases: number of panels with Steps 2+3 time, r_s=.15.

8. Rotate or no rotate panels with Step 3 time, r_s=.34. Non-oral-argument cases: rotate or no rotate panels with Steps 2+3 time, r_s=.67.

9. Tau=.25.

Summary Disposition

Several of the sample courts had developed methods to dispose summarily of some of their cases. They included shortened or no oral argument, bench decisions, disposition by order, and fast-track dockets, among others. The analysis shows that there is a weak relationship between the existence of such mechanisms and disposition time at Step 3: disposition time was shorter in those courts that had a summary disposition method.

Alternative or summary disposition techniques are more successful, with the result of shorter processing time, when steps in the process are eliminated. In other words, methods such as disallowing oral argument or issuing a bench decision (as opposed to a written decision) more effectively shorten processing time than do dockets that merely provide for shortened oral argument.

Appellate judges seem to be ambivalent about oral argument. Many of those interviewed pointed out that attorneys often are ill-prepared, uncomfortable, and inexperienced in arguing cases. They commented that oral argument seldom changed anyone's mind, that it was difficult to schedule (especially in large states, where the geographic jurisdiction of the court was contiguous with the state's boundaries) and time-consuming.

Most of the blame for poor oral argument was directed at attorneys. Some judges stated that it was not uncommon for attorneys merely to read their briefs in oral argument. Though uncomfortable with the practice, some said that on occasion they had accordingly cut off such "oral argument" before expiration of the allotted time. Many said they found oral argument useful in barely ten to fifteen percent of the cases.

Despite these problems, few judges suggested that oral argument be dispensed with entirely in the majority of appellate cases. There is, however, an identifiable trend in the sample courts to shorten oral argument, or, in certain appeals, not to allow it at all. The majority of the judges interviewed were generally satisfied with this trend.

Decisions and Opinions

The decision-making process was similar in all the sample courts. Immediately after oral argument, judges conferred, took a straw vote, and either assigned or confirmed assignment of opinions to particular judges. When opinions were being written, there were usually some informal consultations, at least in courts where judges shared the same facilities. This process was more complex in those jurisdictions where the judges were scattered throughout the state. Judges rarely reconferred formally in fragmented courts. The exception was the Virginia Supreme Court, where the judges attended a formal opinion conference in Richmond, five weeks after arguments were held.

Opinion Content

Though most of the sample courts' opinions were commonly between two and five pages long, several had special rules governing opinion content that could adversely affect both the content and the preparation time of opinions.

It is important to recognize that procedures designed to achieve a goal at one point of the appellate process may have an indirect but nevertheless potentially serious impact on other phases of the process. Policies governing opinion content in the Ohio Court of Appeals, Eighth District, illustrate the dangerous possibilities.

Rule 12 of the Ohio Rules of Appellate Procedure provided in part that "all errors assigned and briefed shall be passed upon by the court in writing, stating the reasons for the court's decision as to each such error." The judges of the court believed that this rule greatly increased their opinion writing time and provided a means for abuse by attorneys attempting to delay the decision process.

The data bear out both of these complaints. Table 6-1 shows that the briefs presented in the Ohio court contained, on the average, more issues than the briefs presented to the other courts in the sample. For example, 17 percent of the appellants' briefs submitted in the Ohio court included eight or more issues, while less than 1 percent of appellants' briefs filed in Oregon, Illinois, and Indiana included that many. It is doubtful that the appeals in Ohio were frequently so much more complex than those in other jurisdictions. It seems more likely that the attorneys in Ohio, having notice of this rule, included superfluous issues in their briefs. In other words, this rule probably had encouraged attorneys to use a shotgun approach in brief preparation. Without the rule requiring separate treatment of every issue briefed, the briefs would probably have contained fewer frivolous and time-consuming issues.

By way of contrast, judges sitting on the Oregon Court of Appeals informally urged attorneys to prepare short briefs, focusing on what the attorneys believed were the crucial issues. Table 6-1 indicates that 76 percent of briefs in that court raised only a single issue, a noticeably different distribution than that in other courts included in this study. Indiana and Illinois also provided an interesting contrast to Ohio. In these states, the courts did not present attorneys with explicit or implicit standards on how many issues briefs should raise, and, in both courts over 90 percent of the briefs raised three issues or less.

Besides regulating content, some courts specify time limits for preparing opinions. In Montana, for example, the writing judge had to submit a draft opinion in 90 days or his pay could be suspended. In Florida, a 90-day rule was also specified, but no sanction was detailed.

Concurring and dissenting opinions appeared infrequently in all of the sample courts. The common reaction of judges was that announcement of a decision more than likely would be delayed if one member of the panel or court wished to submit a concurrence or dissent.

There were too few cases with concurring or dissenting opinions to ascertain statistically the effects that accompanying opinions had on decision time. However, courts with rules governing the timeliness of the preparation of dissents or concurrences generally had shorter decision times than did courts that did not have such rules. In Florida, for example, the Court of Appeal adopted a rule specifying that concurrences and dissents had to be submitted within 30 days after cases had been decided.

Judges' Perceptions of Their Role in the Appellate Process

Judges view their role in the appellate process from different perspectives. One group may view themselves as correcting errors of trial courts. Others may consider their function to be one primarily of setting precedent for future decisions. Still others, of course, may see their role as encompassing both the error-correcting and the precedent-setting functions.

The split between the major perspectives is especially apparent among judges in intermediate appellate courts. Several judges interviewed have expressed strongly the opinion that the need for swift, error-correcting decisions was the reason for the establishment of intermediate appellate courts, and that the setting of judicial precedent was a luxury to be afforded the Supreme Court only. In addition, some intermediate appellate court judges indicated that they were comfortable with the cushion provided by the presence of supreme courts. In contrast, some intermediate court judges (notably those in the Ohio court) submitted that the supreme court in their state granted few petitions for certiorari. Consequently, in practice, for most appeals the intermediate court is in fact a court of last resort and must perform both the error-correcting and the precedent-setting functions.

Supreme court judges from the sample courts (all of which are the only appellate court in the state) expressed the opinion that their role necessarily encompassed both functions. They noted the need for swift, correct decisions when trial courts had erred, but felt quite strongly about the need to give well-reasoned opinions in order to develop the common law of their respective states.

In any event, it is not the task here to examine the philosophical merits of these perspectives. Rather, it is noted that how a court views its role can have an impact on decision time. Specifically, the analysis indicates that courts that view their role primarily as one of correcting error rather than setting precedent generally dispose of their cases faster than do courts adopting the other perspectives. The most extreme example of the former attitude was found in Oregon, where the judicial perception of the court's role as correcting error was expressed most forcefully, and Step 3 time was the shortest.

TABLE 6-1

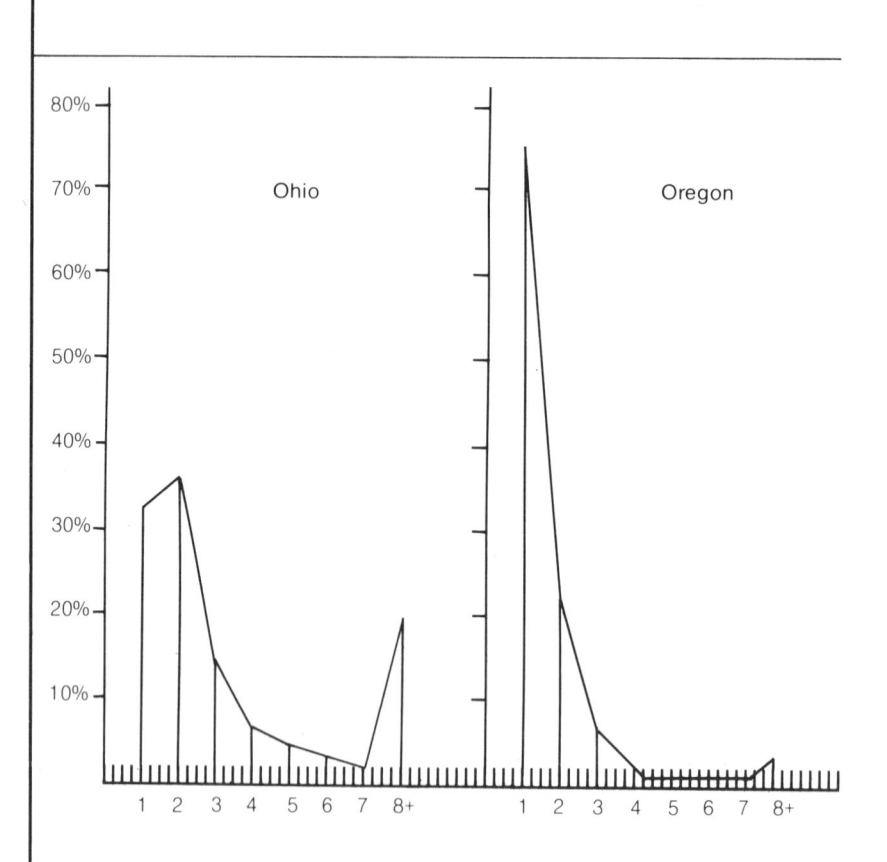

No. of Issues	N (Ohio)	Percent (Ohio)	N (Oregon)	Percent (Oregon)
1	(101)	32	(264)	76
2	(107)	34	(68)	20
3	(39)	12	(13)	4
4	(12)	4	(0)	0
5	(3)	1	(0)	0
6	(1)	.3	(0)	0
7	(0)	0	(0)	0
8+	(52)	17	(1)	.3

Number of Issues Raised by Appellant

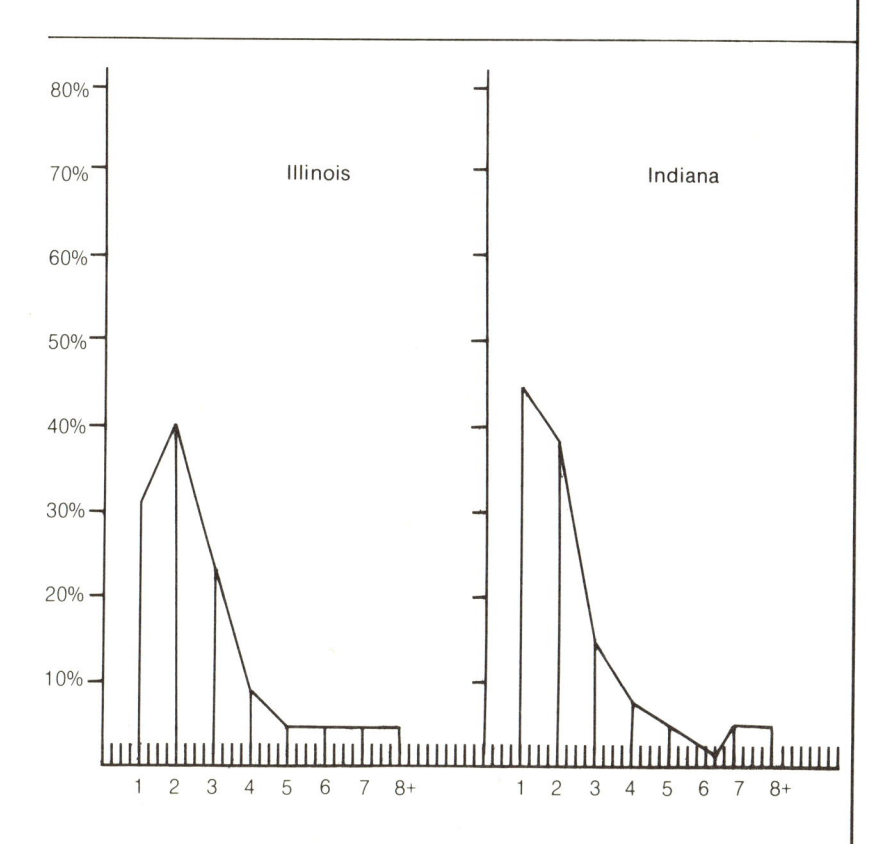

Illinois

N	Percent
(130)	31
(172)	40
(84)	20
(27)	6
(9)	2
(2)	.5
(1)	.2
(2)	.5

Indiana

N	Percent
(171)	43
(149)	37
(58)	15
(13)	3
(8)	2
(0)	0
(1)	.2
(1)	.2

Finally, Step 4, the period between the date a decision is announced and the date the mandate is issued, is in many instances the twilight zone of the appellate process. Few courts exercise control over this final phase. The single most important factor relating to this step in the courts examined was simply whether or not a court was aware of the possibility that delays could occur here. By and large the solution to delay during the final stage is one of establishing uniform clerical procedures for recording mandates.

In a few of the sample courts, mandates were stayed for a designated period, usually betwen 30 to 60 days. Not surprisingly, courts specifying that mandates must remain open usually had longer postdecision time averages than did courts not following such policies.

An Incremental Appellate Reform Strategy 7

Over fifty years have passed since the American educator and social scientist John Dewey suggested that "...thinking and beliefs should be experimental, not absolutist," and that "...policies and proposals for social action be treated as working hypotheses, not as programs to be rigidly adhered to and executed."[1] Dewey's principles and methods provide guidance for contemporary court reform: a foundation on which an incremental appellate court reform strategy can be developed.

When placed within the context of modern appellate court reform, Dewey's precepts imply that citizens and their governmental representatives should allow and even urge appellate courts to undertake willingly a considerable amount of self-examination, to experiment with a variety of possible delay-reducing techniques, and to evaluate rigorously the consequences of the techniques with which they have experimented.

> They [techniques to reduce delay] will be experimental in the sense that they will be entertained subject to constant and well-equipped observation of the consequences they entail when acted upon, and subject to ready and flexible revision in the light of observed consequences.[2]

Philosophy and Method

On a philosophical level, perhaps, judges, administrators, lawyers, legislators, and researchers may recognize the virtues of a reform philosophy of experimentation, evaluation, modification, and change; but in practice there is substantial disparity between Dewey's principles and contemporary appellate court reform.

Currently, techniques that may or may not reduce delay often are

---

[1]. John Dewey, *The Public and Its Problems* (Chicago: Swallow Press, 1954), p. 202. (Originally published by Henry Holt and Co., 1927.)
[2]. Ibid., p. 203.

not regarded as experimental mechanisms. Rather they are viewed as "solutions," often monolithic ones, which should "work," that is, produce the desired effects (preferably immediately) within the context of any appellate system. All too often, contemporary appellate court reform is characterized by a process whereby (a) a court selects and implements a technique or a group of techniques for reducing delay, without first objectively assessing its needs; (b) the techniques are subjectively rather than objectively evaluated; (c) the techniques are either viewed as successes and continued as part of standard procedure in the form originally adopted or are written off as failures and abandoned; and (d) a second court selects and tries a single technique or group of techniques, and the process continues. Three flaws in this model of appellate improvement are evident: first, the selection of a technique without consideration of whether it will actually address the court's problems; second, the lack of objective analysis and documentation in determining the success or failure of any particular technique; and third, the failure of courts to exchange information about their experiences. Thus, under this model, analysis and interchange, fundamental components of serious appellate court reform, are undoubtedly all too often disregarded entirely.

Elements of an Incremental Court Reform Strategy

Before an appellate court can realistically determine the probabilities that any particular delay-reduction technique can meet its needs, prior analysis of its operations and the severity and sources of its delay problems must be undertaken. Each court must address the critical questions of appellate court delay as they relate to its own appellate system. Among these questions are the following:

How long does it take to process cases? What is the average number of elapsed days from judgment in the lower court to final mandate in the appellate court? Are there large variations in elapsed time among cases? How long does each step in the appellate process take? Is there an identifiable relationship between elapsed time in one step and elapsed time in other steps?

When does case processing time constitute delay? Does average time per step in the appellate process exceed the limit stipulated by court rule? Do the rules accurately reflect appellate court expectations?

Can case processing time be reduced? At what points in the process is reduction possible? What are the specific sources of case processing delay?

If case processing time can be shortened, how can that be accomplished? What are the relationships between elements of the court environment and case processing time? Can case processing time be shortened by stricter enforcement of court rules? By increasing resources available to the court? By changes in the environment in which the court operates?

Assessing the Appellate System and Identifying Specific Problems

One approach for assessing the appellate system and identifying its problems is the comprehensive *snapshot* approach used in each of the ten appellate courts included in this study, that is, examining all aspects of a court's operation for a particular group of cases.[3]

The snapshot approach reflects two assumptions: that case processing time is a function of the interactions among cases filed, the organizational aspects of a court, and the actions of its participants, and that a determination of court efficiency must include a detailed assessment of elapsed case processing time during component stages of the appellate process.

The total environment in which the appellate court operates must be considered in analyzing the demands placed on the court and in determining the extent to which the court can adjust its rules and procedures to satisfy more efficiently those demands without enlisting the aid of other governmental units. Environmental elements include constitutional, statutory, and rule provisions, the size of the population served by the court, the geographic location of the court and court personnel, workload as defined by annual filings and backlog, and the resources available to the court.

Reforms designed to reduce case processing time may depend on the alteration of some of those elements that define the general court environment. That is, it may be that in some jurisdictions courts simply do not have the resources necessary to ensure acceptable case processing times, and that efforts to improve the court are dependent on increased court resources. The availability of those resources may be limited by constitutional and statutory provisions or the actions of other governmental branches, such as state legislatures.

The understanding of a court's rules and procedures is another crucial part of any assessment of the sources and severity of delay. Conceptually, rules are an expression of the court's goals, and procedures are means of implementing those goals. Rules serve as a benchmark for assessing the performance of a court: Are the participants meeting the time requirements (goals) set by court rule?

The purpose and content of court rules, as expressions of a court's goals, must be examined. Courts should ask, Are our standards and rules of performance reasonable? If not, what are reasonable stand-

---

3. See specifically, John A. Martin and Elizabeth A. Prescott, *Volume and Delay Staff Study Series*, series editor, Michael J. Hudson (North Andover, Mass.: National Center for State Courts, Northeastern Regional Office).

ards for accomplishing the various steps in our appellate process? Are our rules and standards really performance benchmarks? Similarly, when assessing their appellate systems, courts should ask, Are our rules realistic? Do they reflect our goals within the context of our ability to achieve them? Standards or goals that do not even remotely correspond to the expectations of courts might not serve their purpose of providing models with which individuals can guide and judge their performance. Rather, unrealistic standards might have a negative effect: they may set goals we occasionally think about but largely ignore because they are unattainable.

The work habits of judges and other court personnel can have a great impact on court efficiency, and therefore should be scrutinized. The traditional appellate justice system is characterized by the presence of a few individuals, notably judges, exercising considerable administrative and policy authority. Moreover, analysis by the Appellate Justice Improvement Project revealed that many proposed solutions to delay are contingent on increasing judicial power beyond the formidable levels already existing in the traditional appellate process.

The interaction between the appeals court and other courts, or the nature of the relationships between the appeals court and other courts whose cooperation might be essential for the efficient processing of appeals, is yet another aspect of the appellate system that must be considered. As this analysis revealed, in some jurisdictions examined the lower court judges and clerks controlled the preparation of the record needed by the appeals court, and if their cooperation was lacking, extensive delay could result.

Another element included in the snapshot approach to assessing an appellate system is the court's own perception of delay in the processing of appeals. This perception may be either of specific cases that are considered to require fast disposition or of the caseload as a whole. In the former instance, the perception of urgency can prompt special treatment of the cases in question; in the latter, the perception of systemic delay can prompt both increased individual productivity and a reexamination, and possible revision, of the appellate system.

The types of court record data required to make an assessment of the appellate system as described above include those generally examined in this study—indicators of case types, of case processing time and its components, and of delay:

Substantive content of appeals
—whether the case is a civil or criminal case
—the specific subject matter of the case
—the issues presented as grounds for appeal

Parties to the appeal
—type of appellant
—type of appellee
—status of the parties in the lower court

—type of attorney for appellant
—type of attorney for appellee

Briefs and opinions
—the length of the appellant's brief
—the length of the appellee's brief
—the length of the appellant's reply brief
—the length of the trial court transcript
—the total number of motions during the appeal
—the types of motions during the appeal
—the length of the majority opinion
—the presence or absence of dissenting opinions
—the presence or absence of concurring opinions

Total time: lower court judgment to appellate court mandate
—Lower court judgment to materials submission, including lower court judgment to filing of notice of appeal; notice of appeal to materials submission; filing of transcript to appellant's brief; appellant's brief to appellee's brief; and appellee's brief to appellant's reply brief.
—Materials submission to oral argument
—Oral argument to decision
—Decision to mandate

Selecting and Implementing Techniques for Court Improvement

After a court has examined its appellate system and identified the existence, loci, and severity of its delay problem, it can begin to select delay-reduction techniques. This selection process should include a review of proposed solutions documented in treatises and studies, and discussion with judges and other court personnel in jurisdictions where techniques have been tried, as well as an honest appraisal of the court's own goals, expectations, and environment.

Perhaps most important, courts should recognize that there is simply no single program model for reform applicable to all or even most appellate courts. Even though workable solutions to the problems of delay may be available, no single solution or set of solutions will necessarily solve every court's particular problems.[4] Any reform can be unsuccessful, regardless of the good intentions of all those participating, when placed within the context of a particular appellate court system. Moreover, any reform, no matter how carefully con-

---

4. For a further discussion, see Geoff Gallas, "The Conventional Wisdom of State Court Administration: A Critical Assessment and an Alternative Approach," 2 *Justice System Journal* 35 (Spring 1976), and Carl Baar, "The Scope and Limits of Court Reform," 5 *Justice System Journal* 274 (Spring 1980).

ceived, implemented, and administered, can be subverted by the single or collective actions of judicial system participants, especially the actions of the local bar.

Evaluating Techniques

The remaining components of an incremental appellate reform strategy are a rigorous evaluation of the success or failure of the techniques, and an abandonment or modification of these techniques when necessary. There is a chronic need for a systematic examination of the success or failure of techniques, if serious progress is to be made toward dealing with appellate court delay. Generally, those committed to appellate court reform need more reliable and precise information on the impact of delay-reduction "solutions." Though often eloquently stated, past arguments concerning the desirability and feasibility of certain techniques usually have been but expressions of faith and opinion rather than summaries of scientifically verified fact. There simply have not been rigorously conducted systematic evaluations, let alone experimental investigations, of the actual impact of proposed delay-reduction techniques. As a consequence, appellate court personnel cannot be certain that proposed innovations have really produced the desired effects claimed by their advocates.

There are broader questions that must also be studied for a complete understanding of the appellate process and its problems. Does delay detract from the quality of appellate justice, and if so, how? These questions have not been entertained in this study or addressed adequately elsewhere. Litigants' and attorneys' perceptions of appellate delay also have not been adequately studied. In some instances, delay is undoubtedly advantageous for both. But whether the disadvantages of delay to other lawyers and litigants and to the system itself outweigh those advantages is a question yet unanswered.

Finally, appellate judges' perceptions of delay have not been examined in sufficient detail. Many judges feel that the quality of justice may be diminished by an overemphasis on speed. For example, rapid case processing may deny judges the opportunity to consider cases carefully and to write quality opinions. Whether or not their concerns are justified is simply unknown at this point.

Answering the questions sketched out above and other related crucial questions will undoubtedly require more normative inquiry and detailed empirical investigation. Yet the added effort is justified simply because, as better information is obtained, "...opinion in the sense of beliefs formed and held in absence of evidence will be reduced in quantity and importance. No longer will views generated in view of special situations be frozen into absolute standards and masquerade as eternal truths."[5]

---

5. Dewey, op cit., p. 203.

APPENDIX A

Time Interval Distributions

84 *Appellate Court Delay*

Time Interval Distributions

Statistics describing the distribution of cases for each step in the appellate process in each of the ten sample courts are presented and discussed in this appendix.

While all of the descriptive statistics provide summary information about the nature of distributions, each measure describes distributions in a slightly different way. For example, the first three measures of descriptive statistics included in each table—the mean, median, and mode—are all measures of central tendency or typicality, and are associated with the general notion of "average." The arithmetic mean or average is probably the most widely understood and used measure of central tendency. It is simply the sum of all scores divided by the number of scores. Because the mean can be affected by extreme scores, the median is usually also reported in descriptive tables. The median is the case at the exact midpoint of the distribution—the point or case where one-half of all the cases fall below and one-half above. Finally, the mode is simply the value that occurs most often in a distribution pattern.

The variance and standard deviation are additional measures that describe the distributions of data. Variance is the arithmetic mean of the squared deviations from the mean. (While the concept of variability is of great theoretical consequence to statisticians, it is used here primarily to define standard deviation.) The standard deviation is merely the square root of variance. The size of the standard deviation is inversely proportional to the degree of data concentration about the mean. Consequently, a large standard deviation indicates that data are widely spread and exhibit little central tendency. These two measures are often referred to as measures of dispersion, because, in contrast to measures of central tendency (which describe the typicality of data) these measures describe the heterogeneity of, or variation among, data. Measures of dispersion are particularly important in instances where data do not strongly group around a central value; they indicate that the measures of central tendency, the mean and median, are not representative. Thus, measures of dispersion and central tendency are complementary statistics, the latter describing where the data are grouped, the former describing how widely data are dispersed around this point. For example, applying the principles of central tendency and dispersion to the total case processing time distribution presented in Table A-1, the statistics included in the table indicate that cases cluster closely around the 301-day average (mean) in the Nebraska Supreme Court, but are widely dispersed in the Florida court, as evidenced by the relatively large 274-day standard deviation that accompanies the court's 332-day average.

The third set of statistics included in each table, the confidence interval and the standard error, are measures that help determine how accurately the data from the sample of appellate cases reflect or represent the total caseload. Using information contained in Table A-1 from the Nebraska court once again, we see that the .95 confidence interval statistic indicates a 95 percent probability that the actual mean for all cases (not just the sample) in Nebraska will fall within the approximate range of 292 and 311 days. In other words, if all the cases in the Nebraska Court during the sample years had been included in the data set, there is a 95 percent probability that the total case processing time mean would fall within this extremely narrow range of 292 to 311 days.

Table A-5, which illustrates decision time in non-oral-argument cases, demonstrates how these statistics can be used to identify poor samples. Specifically, the 95 percent confidence interval for data from the Nebraska court indicates a huge range of between 8.7 to 146.9 days and a large standard error of 33.1 days. Figures from the Ohio Court of Appeals sample—standard error equals 24.6; 95 percent confidence interval equals 27.9 to 131.2—also exemplify the utility of these two statistics for identifying a poor sample. Clearly, generalizations made from these two samples could be dangerously misleading.

The final set of statistics contained in each table, the kurtosis and skewness, describe the shape of a graph or curve relative to the ideal bell-shaped curve. Both statistics indicate how closely the actual curve approximates a normal bell-shaped curve, i.e., the skewness indicates whether cases generally cluster to the right or left of the mean, while the kurtosis indicates the "peakness" of the curve. The skewness statistic has a value of zero when the distribution of cases approximates a normal bell-shaped curve, while a positive value means that cases cluster to the left of the mean and a negative value indicates clustering to the right of the mean. A zero value for the kurtosis statistic indicates a normal distribution, a positive value a more "peaked" than normal curve, and a negative value a flatter than normal curve. For example, the skewness and kurtosis statistics presented in Table A-1 indicate that cases in the Nebraska court fall to the left of the mean (or take generally less processing time than would be expected, given a normal distribution) and that the curve is slightly more peaked than normal.

TABLE A-1
Descriptive Statistics:

Court	N	Mean	Median	Mode
Oregon, Court of Appeals	(406)	240	210	167
Nebraska Supreme Court	(603)	301	303	336
Florida Court of Appeal, First District	(337)	332	302	220
Montana Supreme Court	(463)	369	355	405
New Jersey Superior Court, Appellate Division	(395)	378	384	320
Ohio Court of Appeals, Eighth District	(358)	413	481	615
Colorado Court of Appeals	(660)	431	418	489
Virginia Supreme Court	(288)	484	483	437
Indiana Court of Appeals	(338)	641	609	422
Illinois Appellate Court, First District	(311)	648	628	602

Total Case Processing Time

Standard Error	Standard Deviation	Variance	.95 Confidence Interval	Kurtosis	Skew-ness
9.5	191.5	36675.4	221.4 to 258.8	184.9	11.4
4.8	119.6	14323.7	291.7 to 310.8	1.8	.43
14.9	274.0	75115.6	303.4 to 362.1	91.2	7.8
8.3	179.6	32279.9	353.4 to 386.3	1.1	.73
8.3	166.4	27690.2	362.4 to 395.3	.12	.25
11.1	211.1	44585.3	391.5 to 435.40	-.73	-.44
7.5	193.8	37577.6	416.9 to 446.6	2.6	.98
5.9	101.4	10297.6	472.6 to 496.19	2.2	-.53
14.8	272.6	74383.7	611.9 to 670.2	8.1	1.5
14.3	252.1	63580.8	620.4 to 694.5	.34	.37

TABLE A-2
Descriptive Statistics:

Court	N	Mean	Median	Mode
Oregon Court of Appeals	(361)	147	137	122
Nebraska Supreme Court	(390)	204	189	159
Florida Court of Appeal, First District	(333)	179	150	138
Montana Supreme Court	(459)	222	193	83
New Jersey Superior Court, Appellate Division	(319)	271	248	126
Ohio Court of Appeals, Eighth District	(311)	169	142	325
Colorado Court of Appeals	(688)	216	198	140
Virginia Supreme Court*	(349)	70	63	64
Indiana Court of Appeals	(386)	280	258	211
Illinois Appellate Court, First District	(360)	347	302	224

*Statistics for time interval "petition granted to all appeal materials filed."

Step 1, Lower Court Judgment To At Issue

Standard Error	Standard Deviation	Variance	.95 Confidence Interval	Kurtosis	Skewness
2.8	54.3	2949.2	141.6 to 152.9	6.9	1.7
3.7	73.4	5390.1	197.5 to 212.2	11.4	2.3
11.5	210.7	44402.8	156.6 to 202.0	164.7	11.2
6.5	140.6	19789.1	209.2 to 235.0	1.5	1.1
8.6	153.6	23618.4	254.1 to 287.9	.67	.88
5.8	103.1	10631.2	158.3 to 181.3	2.7	1.4
5.9	155.1	24066.5	205.2 to 228.5	79.5	6.1
2.6	49.9	2490.4	65.5 to 76.0	40.1	6.0
7.3	144.8	20968.9	265.6 to 294.6	5.1	1.6
11.6	221.3	48996.7	324.9 to 370.7	1.1	.91

TABLE A-3
Descriptive Statistics:

Court	N	Mean	Median	Mode
Oregon Court of Appeals	(335)	28	21	19
Nebraska Supreme Court	(378)	79	68	133
Florida Court of Appeal, First District	(148)	140	129	79
Montana Supreme Court	(389)	81	72	71
New Jersey Superior Court, Appellate Division	(306)	143	113	90
Ohio Court of Appeals, Eighth District	(278)	263	265	183
Colorado Court of Appeals	(499)	112	102	103
Virginia Supreme Court	(287)	122	113	45
Indiana Court of Appeals	(27)	200	117	60
Illinois Appellate Court, First District	(204)	158	145	98

At Issue To Oral Argument

Standard Error	Standard Deviation	Variance	.95 Confidence Interval	Kurtosis	Skewness
1.7	32.8	1079.8	25.1 to 32.1	74.7	7.0
4.0	78.3	6132.5	75.0 to 87.8	62.1	6.1
5.4	66.0	4363.7	129.5 to 151.0	2.2	.97
2.6	52.7	2786.7	75.7 to 86.3	17.6	3.0
6.1	106.8	11416.9	131.1 to 155.2	8.7	2.3
6.6	111.1	12344.6	250.5 to 276.7	.34	-.13
6.9	155.6	24235.5	98.8 to 126.2	419.2	19.6
4.7	80.5	6491.6	112.8 to 131.5	2.4	1.1
42.9	219.7	48292.8	113.1 to 287.0	5.4	2.1
6.4	92.2	8509.3	145.8 to 171.3	2.3	1.2

TABLE A-4
Descriptive Statistics:

Court	N	Mean	Median	Mode
Oregon Court of Appeals	(334)	24	17	0
Nebraska Supreme Court	(383)	55	43	30
Florida Court of Appeal, First District	(144)	67	29	8
Montana Supreme Court	(411)	66	54	28
New Jersey Superior Court, Appellate Division	(320)	36	15	14
Ohio Court of Appeals, Eighth District	(293)	61	43	85
Colorado Court of Appeals	(507)	72	58	38
Virginia Supreme Court	(288)	64	51	51
Indiana Court of Appeals	(26)	103	55	15
Illinois Appellate Court, First District	(197)	96	59	28

Step 3, Oral Argument To Decision

Standard Error	Standard Deviation	Variance	.95 Confidence Interval	Kurtosis	Skew-mess
1.9	35.9	1290.3	20.2 to 27.9	24.9	3.9
2.5	50.1	2513.3	50.8 to 60.9	64.6	6.5
6.4	77.9	6075.4	54.2 to 79.9	3.1	1.7
2.7	55.7	3111.9	61.3 to 72.1	7.7	2.3
6.1	110.0	12113.4	24.3 to 48.5	181.7	12.4
4.4	75.4	5697.5	53.1 to 70.4	85.5	7.6
2.4	55.8	3115.4	67.6 to 77.4	7.3	2.1
2.5	43.7	1914.5	59.2 to 69.4	42.9	5.9
23.0	117.5	13828.5	56.0 to 151.0	1.1	1.5
14.3	201.5	40637.4	68.4 to 125.1	136.3	10.8

TABLE A-5
Descriptive Statistics:

Court	N	Mean	Median	Mode
Oregon Court of Appeals		Too few cases		
Nebraska Supreme Court	(21)	77	30	20
Florida Court of Appeal, First District	(175)	93	75	44
Montana Supreme Court	(94)	124	77	28
New Jersey Superior Court, Appellate Division	(19)	81	95	0
Ohio Court of Appeals, Eighth District	(19)	79	31	8
Colorado Court of Appeals	(59)	141	136	105
Virginia Supreme Court	(87)	180	134	98
Indiana Court of Appeals	(313)	266	211	63
Illinois Appellate Court, First District	(276)	196	163	98

Steps 2 & 3, Non-Oral Cases, At Issue To Decision

Standard Error	Standard Deviation	Variance	.95 Confidence Interval	Kurtosis	Skew-ness
		Too few cases			
33.1	151.8	23072.1	8.7 to 146.9	18.3	4.1
5.3	70.3	4942.9	82.7 to 103.7	1.9	1.4
14.4	140.3	19710.8	95.3 to 152.8	6.5	2.4
15.7	68.6	4711.3	48.2 to 114.4	-1.3	.26
24.6	107.2	11497.9	27.9 to 131.2	5.6	2.3
7.7	59.2	3511.5	126.1 to 156.9	.9	.82
13.2	123.1	15172.6	154.0 to 206.5	2.9	1.5
10.6	189.1	35789.9	245.5 to 287.6	.05	.83
7.9	132.4	17535.7	180.9 to 212.3	2.3	1.3

TABLE A-6
Descriptive Statistics:

Court	N	Mean	Median	Mode
Oregon Court of Appeals	(328)	55	36	31
Nebraska Supreme Court	(608)	25	21	21
Florida Court of Appeal, First District	(332)	27	17	16
Montana Supreme Court	(322)	19	12	0
New Jersey Superior Court, Appellate Division		Not applicable.*		
Ohio Court of Appeals, Eighth District	(390)	17	11	11
Colorado Court of Appeals	(541)	82	38	19
Virginia Supreme Court	(290)	18	18	0
Indiana Court of Appeals	(328)	85	32	27
Illinois Appellate Court, First District	(422)	112	82	77

*Refer to page xvii. The decision serves as mandate.

Step 4, Decision To Mandate

Standard Error	Standard Deviation	Variance	.95 Confidence Interval	Kurtosis	Skew-ness
2.8	52.3	2737.2	50.0 to 61.4	21.6	4.3
1.4	36.7	1353.2	22.0 to 27.9	343.0	16.4
3.0	54.6	2984.8	21.7 to 33.5	39.5	6.1
2.3	56.0	3146.3	15.1 to 24.4	196.9	12.5
		Not applicable.*			
1.7	34.4	1184.5	14.0 to 20.9	126.0	10.3
4.7	111.0	12333.5	72.9 to 91.7	14.3	3.4
1.7	29.1	848.3	15.2 to 21.9	101.5	8.7
6.7	123.0	15137.1	71.9 to 98.7	45.3	5.2
4.2	87.0	7585.2	104.3 to 120.0	12.3	2.8

APPENDIX B

Delay Statistics

TABLE B-1
Case Processing Time vs. Court Rules and ABA Standards:

Court	N	Court Rule	% Cases Above Rule	% Cases Above Rule + 30 days
Oregon Court of Appeals	(361)	150 days	38	20
Nebraska Supreme Court	(390)	130 days	92	75
Florida Court of Appeal, First District	(333)	145 days	53	37
Montana Supreme Court	(459)	144 days	68	58
New Jersey Superior Court, Appellate Division	(319)	160 days	72	63
Ohio Court of Appeals, Eighth District	(311)	120 days	64	46
Colorado Court of Appeals	(688)	154 days	66	55
Virginia Supreme Court	(349)	79 days*	9	5
Indiana Court of Appeals	(386)	195 days	75	61
Illinois Appellate Court, First District	(360)	177 days	79	72

*Petition granted to all materials filed.

**These standards only measure time from the ordering of the record to at issue. For comparative purposes, 30 days were added to the ABA totals.

Appendix B 101

Step 1, Trial Judgment to at Issue

% Cases Above Rule + 60 days	% Cases Above Rule + 90 days	% Cases Above Rule + 120 days	Days ABA** Standards	% Cases Above ABA Standards
10	4	2	100 civil/ 80 crim.	93 89
50	32	19	100 civil/ 80 crim.	99 99
23	16	10	100 civil/ 80 crim.	78 84
47	40	30	100 civil/ 80 crim.	81 86
58	53	43	100 civil/ 80 crim.	92 94
44	25	20	100 civil/ 80 crim.	77 85
44	32	22	100 civil/ 80 crim.	75 88
3	2	1	Not Applicable	—
42	41	33	100 civil/ 80 crim.	96 94
64	57	51	100 civil/ 80 crim.	88 91

TABLE B-2
Case Processing Time vs. Court Rules and Hypothetical

Court	N	Court Rule	% Cases Above Rule
Oregon Court of Appeals	(269)	Not Specified (90 days)	8
Nebraska Supreme Court	(451)	Not Specified (90 days)	93
Florida Court of Appeal, First District	(220)	140 days	32
Montana Supreme Court	(293)	Not Specified (90 days)	46
New Jersey Superior Court, Appellate Division	(325)	75 days	68
Ohio Court of Appeals, Eighth District	(189)	Not Specified (90 days)	28
Colorado Court of Appeals		Not available from court	
Virginia Supreme Court		Not available from court	
Indiana Court of Appeals	(385)	Not Specified (90 days)	88
Illinois Appellate Court, First District		Insufficient Data	

(90-day hypothetical standard applied to courts that do not specify limits.)

Standards: Step 1A, Lower Court Judgment to Transcript

% Cases Above Rule + 30 days	% Cases Above Rule + 60 days	% Cases Above Rule + 90 days	% Cases Above Rule + 120 days
2	1	0	0
83	68	51	37
22	15	12	10
39	27	19	13
49	40	32	28
18	10	7	5
	Not available from court		
80	64	44	34
	Insufficient Data		

TABLE B-3
Case Processing Time vs. Court Rules and ABA Standards:

Court	N	Court Rule	% Cases Above Rule
Oregon Court of Appeals	(171)	45 days	22
Nebraska Supreme Court	(410)	30 days*	96
Florida Court of Appeal, First District	(166)	30 days*	42
Montana Supreme Court	(399)	30 days	84
New Jersey Superior Court, Appellate Division		Insufficient Data	
Ohio Court of Appeals, Eighth District	(304)	20 days	65
Colorado Court of Appeals	(648)	40 days	76
Virginia Supreme Court	(349)	40 days**	23
Indiana Court of Appeals	(372)	30 days	45
Illinois Appellate Court, First District	(359)	35 days	88

*30 days used for comparison; court rule does not specify time limit.
**Petition granted to brief.

Step 1, Record Received to Appellant Brief

% Cases Above Rule + 30 days	% Cases Above Rule + 60 days	% Cases Above Rule + 90 days	Days ABA Standards	% Cases Above ABA Standards
6	3	1	30 civil / 20 crim.	53 / 89
82	43	13	30 civil / 20 crim.	96 / 98
20	10	4	30 civil / 20 crim.	53 / 77
60	39	20	30 civil / 20 crim.	86 / 90
Insufficient Data				
36	21	13	30 civil / 20 crim.	62 / 74
47	29	24	30 civil / 20 crim.	87 / 92
12	8	1	—	—
28	13	5	30 civil / 20 crim.	53 / 89
70	56	49	30 civil / 20 crim.	93 / 96

Appendix B 105

TABLE B-4
Case Processing Time vs. Court Rules and ABA Standards:

Court	N	Court Rule	% Cases Above Rule
Oregon Court of Appeals	(328)	30 days	54
Nebraska Supreme Court	(396)	30 days	65
Florida Court of Appeal, First District	(289)	20 days	68
Montana Supreme Court	(409)	30 days	75
New Jersey Superior Court, Appellate Division	(316)	30 days	73
Ohio Court of Appeals, Eighth District	(293)	20 days	76
Colorado Court of Appeals	(293)	30 days	66
Virginia Supreme Court	(346)	25 days	23
Indiana Court of Appeals	(341)	30 days	67
Illinois Appellate Court, First District	(322)	35 days	82

Step 1B, Appellant Brief to Appellee Brief

% Cases Above Rule + 30 days	% Cases Above Rule + 60 days	% Cases Above Rule + 90 days	Days ABA Standards	% Cases Above ABA Standards
8	2	1	30 civil/ 20 crim.	64 97
26	3	1	30 civil/ 20 crim.	74 92
22	7	2	30 civil/ 20 crim.	51 64
50	23	12	30 civil/ 20 crim.	82 91
45	27	20	30 civil/ 20 crim.	92
38	20	13	30 civil/ 20 crim.	61 82
27	8	2	30 civil/ 20 crim.	79 86
2	.005	.0028	Not Applicable	
25	12	7	30 civil/ 20 crim.	77 96
64	40	24	30 civil/ 20 crim.	93 98

TABLE B-5
Case Processing Time vs. Hypothetical Standard:

Court	N	Hypothetical Standard	% Cases Above Rule
Oregon Court of Appeals	(335)	60 days	7
Nebraska Supreme Court	(378)	60 days	56
Florida Court of Appeal, First District	(148)	60 days	91
Montana Supreme Court	(389)	60 days	65
New Jersey Superior Court, Appellate Division	(306)	60 days	81
Ohio Court of Appeals, Eighth District	(278)	60 days	94
Colorado Court of Appeals	(499)	60 days	90
Virginia Supreme Court	(287)	60 days	71
Indiana Court of Appeals	(27)	60 days	88
Illinois Appellate Court, First District	(204)	60 days	90

Step 2, at Issue to Oral Argument

% Cases Above Rule + 30 days	% Cases Above Rule + 60 days	% Cases Above Rule + 90 days	% Cases Above Rule + 120 days
3	1	.3	.15
35	19	8	4
77	55	39	22
33	13	6	2
65	46	37	26
92	90	88	82
63	29	11	3
61	47	31	22
59	48	44	30
75	58	47	34

TABLE B-6
Case Processing Time vs. Court Rules and ABA Standards:

Court	N	ABA Average*	% Cases Above ABA Average
Oregon Court of Appeals	(334)	60 days	9
Nebraska Supreme Court	(383)	60 days	31
Florida Court of Appeal, First District	(144)	30 days	49
Montana Supreme Court	(411)	60 days	45
New Jersey Superior Court, Appellate Division	(320)	30 days	33
Ohio Court of Appeals, Eighth District	(293)	30 days	63
Colorado Court of Appeals	(506)	30 days	72
Virginia Supreme Court	(288)	60 days	26
Indiana Court of Appeals	(26)	30 days	69
Illinois Appellate Court, First District	(197)	30 days	81

*Recommended time averages vary according to the size of the decisional unit. Standard 3.52(b)(4).

Step 3, Oral Argument to Decision

ABA Maximum*	% Cases Above ABA Maximum	% Cases Above ABA + 30 days	% Cases Above ABA + 60 days	% Cases Above ABA + 90 days
90 days	3	1	1	.5
90 days	9	5	2	2
60 days	34	28	19	15
90 days	20	12	7	4
60 days	11	8	3	2
60 days	40	17	8	3
60 days	45	26	15	8
90 days	6	4	2	1
60 days	46	35	27	16
60 days	49	28	17	12

TABLE B-7
Case Processing Time vs. ABA Standards: Steps 2 & 3,

Court	N	ABA Average	% Cases Above ABA Average
Oregon Court of Appeals		Insufficient Data	
Nebraska Supreme Court	(21)	60 days	18
Florida Court of Appeal, First District	(175)	30 days	91
Montana Supreme Court	(94)	60 days	61
New Jersey Superior Court, Appellate Division	(19)	30 days	58
Ohio Court of Appeals, Eighth District		Insufficient Data	
Colorado Court of Appeals	(59)	30 days	98
Virginia Supreme Court	(87)	60 days	93
Indiana Court of Appeals	(313)	30 days	99
Illinois Appellate Court, First District	(271)	30 days	95

Materials Received to Decision in Non-Oral-Argument Cases

ABA Maximum	% Cases Above ABA Maximum	% Case Above ABA Maximum + 30 days	% Cases Above ABA Maximum + 60 days	% Cases Above ABA Maximum + 90 days
		Insufficient Data		
90 days	18	10	5	5
60 days	57	38	25	19
90 days	43	33	24	17
60 days	52	52	38	16
		Insufficient Data		
60 days	93	83	63	34
90 days	78	57	45	41
60 days	92	80	72	61
60 days	91	83	68	57

TABLE B-8
Case Processing Time vs. Hypothetical Standard:

Court	N	Hypothetical Standard
Oregon Court of Appeals	(328)	30 days
Nebraska Supreme Court	(608)	30 days
Florida Court of Appeal, First District	(332)	30 days
Montana Supreme Court	(567)	30 days
New Jersey Superior Court, Appellate Division	Not Applicable	
Ohio Court of Appeals, Eighth District	(390)	30 days
Colorado Court of Appeals	(541)	30 days
Virginia Supreme Court	(290)	30 days
Indiana Court of Appeals	(328)	30 days
Illinois Appellate Court, First District	(422)	30 days

Step 4, Decision to Mandate

% Cases Above Standard	% Cases Above Standard + 30 days	% Cases Above Standard + 60 days	% Cases Above Standard + 90 days
97	26	10	5
12	6	1	.3
16	4	2	1
10	4	2	1
	Not Applicable		
7	3	2	1
56	40	31	18
7	1	.01	.01
54	35	28	22
92	87	39	29

Appendix B 115

APPENDIX C

Correlation of Volume with Delay: Summary

TABLE C-1
Summary: Correlation of Volume/Total Time

Total Time: Trial Judgment to Mandate	r_s	Significance Level	r	Significance Level
Filings 1975 with Mean Time	.18	.30	-.04	.44
Filings 1975 with Median Time	.17	.31	-.00	.49
Filings per Judge 1975 with Mean Time	-.22	.26	-.42	.10
Filings per Judge 1975 with Median Time	-.24	.24	-.36	.14
Filings 1976 with Mean Time	-.10	.38	-.11	.37
Filings 1976 with Median Time	-.16	.32	-.08	.41
Filings per Judge 1976 with Mean Time	-.41	.11	-.48	.07
Filings per Judge 1976 with Median Time	-.45	.09	-.44	.09

Correlation of Volume with Delay: Summary

Tables C-1 through C-6 present Spearman's rank-order correlation coefficients (r_S) and Pearson's product-moment correlations (r), which summarize the direction and strength of relationships among measures of case volume, and case processing time and delay.[1]

Statistics Used in the Analysis

Spearman's rho (r_S) is nonparamatic, i.e., it does not require that data are either normally distributed or interval level. Rather, r_S merely requires that data can be rank-ordered or are ordinal in scale. It measures the extent to which one rank ordering corresponds to a second rank ordering. In this study the first set of rankings are measures of volume (e.g., absolute filings 1975 or 1976; filings per judge 1975 or 1976), while the second set are measures of elapsed case processing time and delay. Thus, r_S varies between 1.00 and -1.00, with 1.00 indicating that the two rankings are identical, -1.00 indicating that they are the exact opposites of each other, and 0.00 indicating that there is no positive or negative relationship between the two orderings.

---

1. For a thorough discussion of r and r_S, see Hubert M. Blalock, Jr., *Social Statistics* (New York: McGraw-Hill, 1972), pp. 378-383, 415-418, and Fred N. Kerlinger, *Foundations of Behaviorial Research* (New York: Holt, Rinehart and Winston, 1973), pp. 69, 145-146, 202-213, 294.

TABLE C-2
Summary: Correlation of Volume/Materials-Preparation Time

STEP 1: Trial Judgment to Materials Received	r_s	Significance Level	r	Significance Level
Elapsed Time				
Filings 1975 with Mean Time	.04	.45	.22	.26
Filings 1975 with Median Time	.07	.41	.19	.29
Filings 1976 with Mean Time	-.15	.33	.15	.33
Filings 1976 with Median Time	-.11	.37	.14	.34
Filings per Judge 1975 with Mean Time	-.45	.09	-.47	.08
Filings per Judge 1975 with Median Time	-.41	.11	-.44	.10
Filings per Judge 1976 with Mean Time	-.60	.03	-.52	.06
Filings per Judge 1976 with Median Time	-.55	.05	-.47	.08
Percent Cases Exceeding Court Rules				
Filings 1975	-.13	.35	-.06	.42
Filings 1976	-.33	.17	-.10	.38
Filings per Judge 1975	-.66	.01	-.54	.05
Filings per Judge 1976	-.72	.01	-.57	.04
Percent Cases Exceeding Rules + 60 Days				
Filings 1975	.20	.29	.17	.31
Filings 1976	-.05	.44	.10	.38
Filings per Judge 1975	-.42	.11	-.54	.05
Filings per Judge 1976	-.54	.05	-.60	.03

Although there are no set mathematical criteria for labeling the strengths of r_s, we followed the conventional standards used in social science literature. These standards classify .00 to .15 positive or negative as non-significant relationships, .16 to .29 positive or negative as weak relationships, .30 to .45 positive or negative as moderately strong relationships, and .46 to 1.00 positive or negative as strong relationships.[2]

The Pearson correlation coefficient (r), similar to r_s, is also used to measure the strength of relationships between two variables. Unlike r_s, r requires interval-level variables, and the strength of relationship indicates both the goodness of fit of a linear regression line to the data

---

[2]. See for example Robert V. Stover and Dennis R. Eckart, "A Systematic Comparison of Public Defenders and Private Attorneys," 3 *American Journal of Criminal Law* 265, Winter, 1975.

120 Appellate Court Delay

TABLE C-3
Summary: Correlation of Volume/Waiting Time

STEP 2: Materials to Oral Argument	r_s	Significance Level	r	Significance Level
Elapsed Time				
Filings 1975 with Mean Time	.51	.06	.18	.30
Filings 1975 with Median Time	.60	.03	.21	.28
Filings 1976 with Mean Time	.24	.24	.13	.35
Filings 1976 with Median Time	.35	.15	.14	.34
Filings per Judge 1975 with Mean Time	.18	.30	.17	.31
Filings per Judge 1975 with Median Time	.36	.14	.32	.18
Filings per Judge 1976 with Mean Time	-.04	.45	.07	.41
Filings per Judge 1976 with Median Time	.11	.37	.20	.28
Percent Cases Exceeding 60 Days				
Filings 1975	.47	.08	.13	.35
Filings 1976	.29	.20	.07	.42
Filings per Judge 1975	.38	.13	-.07	.41
Filings per Judge 1976	.21	.35	-.16	.32
Percent Cases Exceeding 90 Days				
Filings 1975	.69	.01	.30	.19
Filings 1976	.50	.07	.23	.25
Filings per Judge 1975	.55	.13	.23	.25
Filings per Judge 1976	.35	.15	.13	.36
Percent Cases Exceeding 120 Days				
Filings 1975	.55	.05	.32	.17
Filings 1976	.30	.198	.26	.23
Filings per Judge 1975	.40	.12	.38	.13
Filings per Judge 1976	.16	.32	.27	.22

and the proportion of variance in one variable explained by the other (when r is squared). Moreover, the values of r generally will be slightly lower than the values of r_s.

In order to satisfy numerous statistics-based considerations, both r and r_s were used in this analysis. For example, arguments can be made that both measures of absolute volume and volume per judge form interval scales, and hence r would be the appropriate statistic to use. One could also argue that absolute filings and filings per judge are only approximations of workload (that 5 filings in court X do not equal 5

TABLE C-4
Summary: Correlation of Volume/Decision Time

STEP 2: Materials to Oral Argument	r_s	Significance Level	r	Significance Level
Elapsed Time				
Filings 1975 with Mean Time	-.22	.26	-.42	.11
Filings 1975 with Median Time	-.34	.16	-.63	.02
Filings 1976 with Mean Time	-.35	.15	-.48	.08
Filings 1976 with Median Time	-.57	.04	-.69	.01
Filings per Judge 1975 with Mean Time	-.41	.11	-.50	.07
Filings per Judge 1975 with Median Time	-.56	.04	-.66	.01
Filings per Judge 1976 with Mean Time	-.53	.05	-.54	.05
Filings per Judge 1976 with Median Time	-.67	.01	-.71	.01
Percent Cases Exceeding ABA Average				
Filings 1975	.15	.33	-.17	.31
Filings 1976	.30	.19	-.25	.23
Filings per Judge 1975	.40	.12	-.36	.14
Filings per Judge 1976	.16	.32	-.44	.09
Percent Cases Exceeding ABA Maximum				
Filings 1975	.13	.35	-.19	.29
Filings 1976	-.09	.40	-.26	.23
Filings per Judge 1975	-.21	.27	-.22	.26
Filings per Judge 1976	-.38	.13	-.28	.21
Percent Cases Exceeding ABA Maximum + 30 Days				
Filings 1975	.07	.41	-.19	.29
Filings 1976	-.10	.38	-.23	.25
Filings per Judge 1975	-.23	.25	-.20	.28
Filings per Judge 1976	-.41	.11	-.24	.25

TABLE C-5
Summary: Correlation of Decision Time/ Non-Oral-Argument Cases

STEPS 2 & 3: Materials to Decision	r_s	Significance Level	r	Significance Level
Elapsed Time				
Filings 1975 with Mean Time	-.05	.45	-.30	.20
Filings 1975 with Median Time	.11	.38	-.05	.44
Filings 1976 with Mean Time	-.08	.41	-.32	.19
Filings 1976 with Median Time	.05	.45	-.06	.43
Filings per Judge 1975 with Mean Time	-.26	.24	-.46	.10
Filings per Judge 1975 with Median Time	-.28	.23	-.40	.14
Filings per Judge 1976 with Mean Time	-.41	.13	-.45	.11
Filings per Judge 1976 with Median Time	-.41	.13	-.38	.15

filings in court Y) and that consequently the sample courts' caseloads can be only roughly ordered or formed in ordinal scale. In any event, both statistics are supplied for readers to examine.

A second statistic (derived from Student's t with N-2 degrees of freedom from the computed quantity) appears under the "significance level" category accompanying each correlation reported in Tables C-1 through C-6.[3] This statistic indicates the probability that the relationship summarized by the r or r_S is due to sampling error. An accompanying .05 significance level value indicates that the relationship summarized by r or r_S has one-twentieth of a chance of being attributable to sampling error. A value of .01 indicates that the possibility of the relationship being attributable to sampling error is one in a hundred. Because the correlations presented in Tables C-1 through C-6 are based on data from a relatively small sample of only ten courts, the significance level statistics will tend to be large, unless strong relationships exist. From a practical standpoint, this indicates that caution should be exercised when interpreting the correlations, i.e., the results should not be over-generalized.

Correlation Results

Correlations presented in Tables C-1 through C-6 indicate that when r_S is computed, it makes little difference whether each court's

---

3. See Norman Nie et al., *Statistical Package for the Social Sciences* (New York: McGraw-Hill, 1975), pp. 267-271, 281, for a more complete discussion of Student's t.

TABLE C-6
Summary: Correlation of Volume/Post-decision Time

STEP 4: Decision to Mandate	r_s	Significance Level	r	Significance Level
Elapsed Time:				
Filings 1975 with Mean Time	.13	.36	.13	.36
Filings 1975 with Median Time	.16	.33	.36	.16
Filings 1976 with Mean Time	.16	.33	.03	.46
Filings 1976 with Median Time	.18	.31	.22	.28
Filings per Judge 1975 with Mean Time	-.23	.27	-.44	.11
Filings per Judge 1975 with Median Time	-.15	.34	-.33	.19
Filings per Judge 1976 with Mean Time	-.26	.24	-.45	.10
Filings per Judge 1976 with Median Time	-.14	.35	-.36	.16
Percent Cases Above 30 Days				
Filings 1975	.20	.29	.28	.22
Filings 1976	.35	.17	.26	.24
Filings per Judge 1975	-.01	.48	-.16	.33
Filings per Judge 1976	.02	.47	-.13	.36
Percent Cases Above 60 Days				
Filings 1975	.06	.43	.27	.23
Filings 1976	.01	.48	.13	.36
Filings per Judge 1975	-.33	.37	-.40	.13
Filings per Judge 1976	-.35	.17	-.44	.11

case processing time average or its median is used for rank-ordering. Both measures lead to approximately the same results. For example, as indicated by the first two correlations in Table C-1 (when the relationship between 1975 filings and case processing time is examined), if the mean is used as the measure of time, r_S=.18, while if the median is used, r_S=.17. The same general pattern of relative uniformity between results based on either the mean or the median is also apparent for the r statistics. Thus the findings reported in Chapter 4, which are based on using mean case processing time, would be essentially the same if the median had been reported.

Although generally there is little disparity between results when r as opposed to r_S is used (i.e., relationships that emerged when r_S was used do not disappear when r is used), there are a few noteworthy inconsistencies. Specifically, data presented in Table C-3 reveal considerable disparity among the magnitudes of r_S and r. Generally, the r_s statistics indicate moderate or even strong positive relationships between absolute case volume (filings) and case processing time attributable to Step 2 of the appellate process, yet the r statistics indicate weak or no significant positive relationships. While we cannot be certain, these disparities probably are due to the fact that r_s is based on a simple rank order, and consequently cannot fully capture the considerable magnitude of differences in case filings among the sample courts. The second statistics, r, on the other hand are interval based and hence would more fully reflect the magnitudes of differences in filings among the sample courts.

APPENDIX D

Case-Characteristics Breakdowns

Case-Characteristics Breakdowns

The format used in Table D-1 and all other tables in this appendix is slightly different from that of Table 4-3 (see page 43). Table D-1 presents the means and standard deviations for only the upper and lower extremes of case-characteristics categories. This simplified format was adopted for readability. If means, standard deviations, and numbers of cases for all of the case categories, for all ten sample courts, were included in a single table, the table would be both too long and needlessly complex. For example, criminal and civil cases were classified under 38 distinct categories (20 criminal and 18 civil). If all the sample courts were included, the table would report a minimum of 1,140 (38 means, 38 standard deviations, and 38 "n's" per court) and require at least nine pages to present. See *Volume and Delay in Appellate Courts: Some Preliminary Findings From a National Study,* by Steven Weller, John A. Martin, and Elizabeth A. Prescott (Williamsburg, Va.: National Center for State Courts, 1980), pages 72-133 and Appendix Tables A-1 to A-53, for a complete version of Table D-1 and all other case-characteristics tables included in this appendix. The statistical analysis of differences among case categories reported in Chapter 4 was, of course, based on all the categories included in the variable, not just the extreme categories.

TABLE D-1
Total Case Processing Time Variation: Criminal and Civil

Jurisdiction	Upper Extreme N	Mean	S.D.	Lower Extreme N	Mean	S.D.	Significance Level
Criminal Subject Matter							
Indiana Court of Appeals	*Manslaughter* (4)	962 days	462	*Burglary* (32)	505 days	148	.05
Illinois Appellate Court, First District	*Murder II* (6)	817 days	271	*Criminal Trespass* (2)	259 days	23	.01

(Eight remaining courts: no statistically discernible differences between categories.)

Civil Subject Matter							
Florida Court of Appeal, First District	*Taxes* (5)	787 days	975	*Other Administrative Law* (18)	263 days	181	.01
Ohio Court of Appeals, Eighth District	*Other Administrative Law* (8)	499 days	151	*Landlord-Tenant* (3)	335 days	381	.01
Indiana Court of Appeals	*Non-Auto Injury* (13)	764 days	284	*Election Disputes* (3)	326 days	260	.05
Montana Supreme Court	*Election Disputes* (1)	1078 days	0	*Landlord-Tenant* (1)	271 days	0	.01
Colorado Court of Appeals	*Auto Injury* (20)	504 days	211	*Workmen's Compensation* (29)	256 days	100	.001
Oregon Court of Appeals	*Zoning* (4)	453 days	152	*Other Domestic Relations* (15)	201 days	123	.001

(Four remaining courts: no statistically discernible differences among categories.)

TABLE D-2
Total Case Processing Time Variation: Primary Issue Raised on Appeal

Jurisdiction	Upper Extreme N	Mean	S.D.	Lower Extreme N	Mean	S.D.	Significance Level
	\multicolumn{7}{c}{Criminal Subject Matter}
	Insufficient Evidence			Excessive Fine or Sentence			
New Jersey Superior Court, Appellate Division	(29)	472 days	125	(3)	325 days	155	.01
	Erroneous Jury Instructions			Rights Violation			
Nebraska Supreme Court	(6)	403 days	70	(6)	272 days	126	.001
	Erroneous Jury Instructions			Unconstitutional Statute or Ordinance			
Montana Supreme Court	(9)	465 days	125	(5)	258 days	198	.001
	Erroneous Jury Instructions			Unconstitutional Money Judgment			
Colorado Court of Appeals	(29)	560 days	148	(33)	384 days	128	.05

(Six remaining courts: no statistically discernible differences among categories.)

TABLE D-3
Total Case Processing Time Variation: Number of Issues and Subject Matters

Jurisdiction	No. Civil Subjects N	r_s	No. Criminal Subjects N	r_s	No. Issues Appellant N	r_s	No. Issues Appellee N	r_s
Oregon Court of Appeals	(229)	-.05	(167)	.11	(326)	.09	(403)	.06
Nebraska Supreme Court	(324)	-.02	(278)	.04	(406)	.18	(31)	-.06
Florida Court of Appeal, First District	(161)	-.09	(151)	.07	(220)	.05	(317)	.09
Montana Supreme Court	(362)	.03	(82)	.03	(348)	.24	(452)	-.01
New Jersey Superior Court, Appellate Division	(230)	-.00	(141)	.07	(378)	-.20	(378)	-.06
Ohio Court of Appeals, Eighth District	(162)	-.02	(132)	-.03	(232)	.05	(89)	.22
Colorado Court of Appeals	(444)	.11	(168)	.03	(553)	.08	(567)	-.13
Virginia Supreme Court	(264)	-.04	(108)	.10	(276)	.09	(269)	.09
Indiana Court of Appeals	(174)	.08	(167)	.03	(323)	.14	(336)	.09
Illinois Appellate Court, First District	(133)	.00	(170)	.15	(287)	.23	(303)	.01

TABLE D-4
Total Case Processing Time Variation: Type of Litigant

Jurisdiction	Upper Extreme N / Mean / S.D.	Lower Extreme N / Mean / S.D.	Significance Level
Appellant Type			
New Jersey Superior Court, Appellate Division	Government Agency (3) 622 days 213	Interest Group (8) 269 days 144	.05
Florida Court of Appeal, First District	The State (6) 752 days 877	Government Agency (11) 318 days 152	.01
Ohio Court of Appeals, Eighth District	Municipalities (46) 535 days 159	Interest Group (2) 290 days 136	.001
Nebraska Supreme Court	Government Agency (13) 388 days 105	The State (10) 226 days 123	.001
Oregon Court of Appeals	The State (25) 370 days 646	Individual (345) 226 days 101	.01

(Five remaining courts: no statistically significant differences among categories.)

Appellee Type			
Indiana Court of Appeals	Multiple Individuals (20) 818 days 322	Government Agency (11) 513 days 372	.05
Illinois Appellate Court, First District	Multiple Individuals (17) 695 days 236	Municipalities (5) 538 days 86	.05
Nebraska Supreme Court	Other Not Easily Classified (8) 446 days 250	The State (267) 261 days 94	.001

(continued on next page)

Jurisdiction	Upper Extreme N	Mean	S.D.	Lower Extreme N	Mean	S.D.	Significance Level
	Appellee Type						
	The State			Other Not Easily Classified			
Montana Supreme Court	(80)	438 days	187	(3)	237 days	208	.01
	The State			Government Agencies			
Colorado Court of Appeals	(185)	514 days	190	(66)	306 days	150	.001
	Multiple Individuals			Business			
Oregon Court of Appeals	(2)	414 days	58	(12)	183 days	78	.01

(Four remaining courts: no statistically significant differences among categories.)

TABLE D-5
Total Case Processing Time Variation: Type of Attorney

Jurisdiction	Upper Extreme N	Mean	S.D.	Lower Extreme N	Mean	S.D.	Significance Level
Appellant Attorney							
	Public Defender			*Pro Se*			
New Jersey Superior Court, Appellate Division	(101)	423 days	183	(4)	229 days	196	.05
	Attorney General			*Pro Se*			
Florida Court of Appeal, First District	(6)	712 days	895	(18)	225 days	122	.01
	Municipal Corp. Counsel			*Attorney General*			
Ohio Court of Appeals, Eighth District	(40)	552 days	139	(5)	314 days	200	.001
	Attorney General			*District Attorney*			
Nebraska Supreme Court	(12)	363 days	128	(9)	219 days	120	.001
	Public Defender			*Pro Se*			
Colorado Court of Appeals	(111)	540 days	175	(13)	288 days	137	.001
	Attorney General			*Pro Se*			
Oregon Court of Appeals	(29)	348 days	604	(6)	185 days	110	.05

(Four remaining courts: no statistically significant differences between categories.)

Appellee Attorney							
	Public Defender			*Pro Se*			
Illinois Appellate Court, First District	(2)	1049 days	38	(2)	394 days	52	.01
	Municipal Corp. Counsel			*Public Defender*			
Nebraska Supreme Court	(25)	376 days	118	(4)	159 days	156	.001

(continued on next page)

Jurisdiction	Upper Extreme			Lower Extreme			Significance Level
	N	Mean	S.D.	N	Mean	S.D.	
		**Appellee Attorney**					
	colspan="3"	Public Defender		Attorney General		
Montana Supreme Court	(2)	496 days	482	(36)	269 days	156	.05
	colspan="3"	District Attorney		Legal Aid		
Colorado Court of Appeals	(16)	543 days	216	(2)	210 days	282	.05

(Six remaining courts: no statistically significant differences between categories.)

TABLE D-6
Total Case Processing Time Variation: Number of Parties Per Case

Jurisdiction	Total No. of Appellants N	r_s	Total No. of Appellees N	r_s
Oregon Court of Appeals	(383)	.08	(229)	-.05
Nebraska Supreme Court	(598)	.14	(597)	-.29
Florida Court of Appeal, First District	(335)	.09	(333)	-.16
Montana Supreme Court	(431)	-.03	(423)	.13
New Jersey Superior Court, Appellate Division	(395)	-.12	(394)	.05
Ohio Court of Appeals, Eighth District	(358)	.22	(356)	.08
Colorado Court of Appeals	(654)	.02	(654)	.21
Virginia Supreme Court	(284)	.05	(282)	-.03
Indiana Court of Appeals	(322)	.08	(315)	-.06
Illinois Appellate Court, First District	(303)	.06	(305)	.12

TABLE D-7
Total Case Processing Time Variation: Number of Time Extensions

Jurisdiction	Total No. of Motions N	r_s
Oregon Court of Appeals	(406)	.36
Nebraska Supreme Court	(531)	.30
Florida Court of Appeal, First District	(337)	.36
Montana Supreme Court	(463)	.57
New Jersey Superior Court, Appellate Division	Not Available	
Ohio Court of Appeals, Eighth District	(353)	.35
Colorado Court of Appeals	(642)	.58
Virginia Supreme Court	(281)	.31
Indiana Court of Appeals	(338)	.26
Illinois Appellate Court, First District	(311)	.53

TABLE D-8
Total Case Processing Time Variation: Characteristics of the Opinion

Jurisdiction	Length of Majority Opinion N	Correlation	Concurring vs. No Concurring Opinions N	Correlation	Dissenting vs. No Dissenting Opinions N	Correlation
Oregon Court of Appeals	(191)	.37	(235)	.05	(235)	.15
Nebraska Supreme Court	(385)	.34	(389)	.13	(392)	.14
Florida Court of Appeal, First Distict	(291)	.23	(320)	-.11	(321)	.11
Montana Supreme Court	(435)	.39	(445)	.18	(448)	.13
New Jersey Superior Court, Appellate Division			Not Available			
Ohio Court of Appeals, Eighth District	(209)	.32	(204)	.01	(206)	.03
Colorado Court of Appeals	(533)	.31	(556)	.04	(556)	.05
Virginia Supreme Court	(282)	.28	(282)	.01	(282)	.02
Indiana Court of Appeals	(318)	.22	(334)	.02	(336)	.06
Illinois Appellate Court, First District	(249)	.36	(295)	.03	(294)	.05

APPENDIX E

Uniform Data-Collection Instrument

Name _____

COURT RECORD DATA

1. Name of Court _____
2. Docket number in this Court _____
3. Short title of case in this Court _____

4. Names of Principal Parties
   (a) Name of appellant (or, if not an appeal, name of party asking court to consider the matter) _____
       (1) _____ Plaintiff below (if applicable)
       (2) _____ Defendant below (if applicable)
   (b) Name of appellee (or, if not an appeal, name of party in position of defendant or respondent) _____
       (1) Plaintiff below (if applicable)
       (2) Defendant below (if applicable)
   (c) Name and status (with respect to this case) of any other principal parties to the case
       (1) _____
       (2) _____
       (3) _____
       (4) _____
   (d) Was there a cross appeal?
       (1) _____ Yes (2) _____ No
   (e) Were there any intervenors?
       (1) _____ Yes (2) _____ No (3) If yes, how many? _____
   (f) Were any amicus curiae briefs filed?
       (1) _____ Yes (2) _____ No (3) If yes, how many? _____
   (g) Was this case consolidated with any other cases pending before the court?
       (1) _____ Yes (2) _____ No (3) If yes, how many? _____

5. Attorneys
   (a) Name of attorney for appellant (or other party listed in answer to 4(a) above) _____
       Check one:
       _____ (1) Private Counsel   _____ (4) Municipal Corp. Counsel
       _____ (2) Attorney General   _____ (5) Public Defender
       _____ (3) District Attorney   _____ (6) Legal Aid
                                          _____ (7) Other
   (b) Name of attorney for appellee (or other party listed in answer to 4(b) above) _____
       Check one:
       _____ (1) Private Counsel   _____ (4) Municipal Corp. Counsel
       _____ (2) Attorney General   _____ (5) Public Defender
       _____ (3) District Attorney   _____ (6) Legal Aid
                                          _____ (7) Other

6. **Source of Case** (check one)
   (a) _____ Appeal from final judgment of trial court
       (1) Name of Trial Court _____
       (2) Trial Court Docket Number _____
   (b) _____ Interlocutory appeal from trial court order
       (1) Name of Trial Court _____
   (c) _____ Review of administrative agency order
       (1) Name of Agency _____
   (d) _____ Original Jurisdiction (Type _____)
   (e) _____ Other (Specify _____)

7. **Type of Jurisdiction**
   (a) _____ Mandatory   (b) _____ Discretionary

8. **Category of Case**
   (a) _____ Criminal
       (1) _____ Direct appeal from conviction—adult
       (2) _____ Direct appeal from judgment—juvenile delinquency
       (3) _____ Collateral attack (post-conviction remedy proceeding)
   (b) _____ Non-criminal

9. **Civil Cases—Disposition**
   (a) Method of disposition
       (1) _____ Dismissal of Complaint or Petition
       (2) _____ Summary judgment for Appellant
       (3) _____ Summary judgment for Appellee
       (4) _____ Judgment at trial for Appellant
       (5) _____ Judgment at trial court Appellee
       (6) _____ Other (Specify _____)
   (b) Relief at issue in forum below (check all that apply)
       (1) _____ Money judgment
       (2) _____ Specific performance
       (3) _____ Injunction
       (4) _____ Other (Specify _____)

10. **Criminal Cases—Disposition**
    (a) Method of disposition below
        (1) _____ Dismissal of charges
        (2) _____ Guilty plea
        (3) _____ Verdict of not guilty at trial
        (4) _____ Verdict of guilty at trial
        (5) _____ Judgment in post-conviction remedy proceeding
            (Specify type _____)
            _____ (a) Relief granted
            _____ (b) Relief denied
        (6) _____ Other (Specify _____)
    (b) Sentence, if judgment below was plea of guilty or verdict of guilty after trial.
        (1) _____ Defendant fined (Amount: $_____)
        (2) _____ Defendant imprisoned (Term: _____)
        (3) _____ Defendant given probation
        (4) _____ Other (Specify _____)

140   Appellate Court Delay

11. Is this case on appeal from a judgment after a jury trial?
    (a) Yes _____   (b) No _____
12. If the case is a criminal case, was defendant incarcerated during appellate court proceedings?
    (a) Yes _____   (b) No _____
13. Civil Cases—Subject Matter of Case (check all that apply)
    (a) _____ Administrative Law Cases
        (1) _____ Liquor
        (2) _____ Motor Vehicle
        (3) _____ Workmen's Compensation
        (4) _____ Elections
        (5) _____ Taxes (Specify type _____)
        (6) _____ Other (Specify _____)
    (b) _____ Other Civil Cases
        (1) _____ Commercial transactions (including contract but not including property)
        (2) _____ Property
            (a) _____ Landlord-tenant
            (b) _____ Other property case not involving administrative agency
        (3) _____ Domestic relations
            (a) _____ Child custody or support
            (b) _____ Juvenile (except juvenile delinquency)
            (c) _____ Other domestic relations
        (4) _____ Injury to persons or property
            (a) _____ Auto
            (b) _____ Other
        (5) _____ Labor relations (including public employees)
        (6) _____ Other (Specify _____)
14. Criminal Cases—Offense Involved (check all that apply)
    (a) _____ First degree murder   (g) _____ Arson
    (b) _____ Second degree murder   (h) _____ Criminal trespass
    (c) _____ Rape or other sexual assault   (i) _____ Sale or possession of narcotics
    (d) _____ Robbery   (j) _____ Drunkenness
    (e) _____ Assault   (k) _____ Disorderly conduct
    (f) _____ Fraud or embezzlement   (l) _____ Traffic
    (m) _____ Juvenile delinquency (Specify offense(s) _____
    _____)
    (n) _____ Other (Specify _____)
15. Were any of the following issues raised as grounds for appeal? (check all that apply)

	By Appel-lant(s)	On Cross Appeal
(1) Misconduct of judge or attorney at trial	_____	_____
(2) Evidence insufficient to support verdict	_____	_____
(3) Erroneous ruling admitting or excluding evidence	_____	_____
(4) Erroneous instructions to jury	_____	_____
(5) Excessive money judgment (civil cases)	_____	_____

(6) Insufficient money judgment (civil cases)   _____ _____
(7) Excessive fine or sentence (criminal cases)   _____ _____
(8) Denial of a person's constitutional rights   _____ _____
(9) Erroneous interpretation of law   _____ _____
(10) Statute/ordinance unconstitutional   _____ _____

16. **Length of Briefs**
    (a) Appellant's: _____ pages   (c) Appellant's reply: _____ pages
    (b) Appellee's: _____ pages   (d) Other (longest): _____ pages

17. **Disposition**
    (a) _____ Voluntary dismissal or withdrawal by appellant or by joint stipulation
    (b) _____ Dismissal on motion of appellee
    (c) _____ Dismissal on court's own motion
    (d) _____ Discretionary review denied
    (e) _____ Affirmed
    (f) _____ Reversed
    (g) _____ Other (Specify _____)

18. **Opinion(s)**
    (a) Majority opinion
        (1) Name of author _____
        (2) No. of pages: _____
    (b) Were there any concurring opinions?
        (1) _____ Yes (Number _____)   (2) _____ No
    (c) Were there any dissenting opinions?
        (1) _____ Yes (Number _____)   (2) _____ No
    (d) Was or were the opinion(s) published?
        (1) _____ Published   (2) _____ Unpublished

19. **Time Lapse Data**
    (a) Basic steps (enter dates)   Date
        (1) Judgment or order being appealed   _____
        (2a) If non-discretionary case:
            (a) Initiation of appeal or proceeding   _____
        (2b) If exercise of discretionary power to review:
            (a) Petition for review filed   _____
            (b) Brief in support of petition filed   _____
            (c) Brief in opposition to petition filed   _____
            (d) Petition for review granted/denied   _____
        (3) Trial court record received   _____
        (4) Trial transcript ordered   _____
        (5) Trial transcript received   _____
        (6) Appellant's main brief filed   _____
        (7) Appellee's main brief filed   _____
        (8) Appellant's reply brief filed   _____
        (9) Other briefs filed (last one)   _____
        (10) Oral argument   _____
        (11) Decision announced   _____
        (12) Petition for rehearing filed   _____
        (13) Petition for rehearing decided   _____
        (14) Issuance of mandate   _____

(b) Other steps
  (1) Was there a central staff review?
      Yes _____   No _____
      If yes, date sent to staff   _____
      Date review completed   _____
  (2) Was there a prehearing settlement?
      Yes _____   No _____
      If yes, date of conference   _____
  (3) Other significant steps
      _____   _____
      _____   _____
      _____   _____

20. **Length of Trial Court Transcript:** _____ (pages)

21. **Motions**

   (a) Moving party   _____   Date: _____
       Subject   _____
       Decided by: _____
       Disposition   _____   Date: _____

   (b) Moving party   _____   Date: _____
       Subject   _____
       Decided by: _____
       Disposition   _____   Date: _____

   (c) Moving party   _____   Date: _____
       Subject   _____
       Decided by: _____
       Disposition   _____   Date: _____

   (d) Moving party   _____   Date: _____
       Subject   _____
       Decided by: _____
       Disposition   _____   Date: _____

   (e) Moving party   _____   Date: _____
       Subject   _____
       Decided by: _____
       Disposition   _____   Date: _____

   (f) Moving party   _____   Date: _____
       Subject   _____
       Decided by: _____
       Disposition   _____   Date: _____

   (g) Moving party   _____   Date: _____
       Subject   _____
       Decided by: _____
       Disposition   _____   Date: _____

Appendix E   *143*

(h) Moving party   _____   Date: _____
     Subject   _____
     Decided by: _____
     Disposition   _____   Date: _____

(i) Moving party   _____   Date: _____
     Subject   _____
     Decided by: _____
     Disposition   _____   Date: _____

22. **Notes and Comments**

AFTERWORDS

Anne N. Costain
Robert A. Leflar
Alfred Blumstein

Reducing Delay in Government Institutions
Comments on
Appellate Court Delay

Professor Anne N. Costain
Department of Political Science, University of Colorado

The study of volume and delay in the appellate courts by John Martin and Elizabeth Prescott has systematically and carefully presented a body of data that challenges many of our most cherished notions of how to speed up decision making in governmental organizations. First, it raises questions about a major premise of much work on delay, namely, that delay is caused when the volume of work in an organization begins to exceed the capability of existing personnel to handle it effectively. In a judicial context this suggests that as the caseload of each judge rises, at some point the ability of the judge and his staff to process these cases will be exceeded and delay will result. From this simple definition of delay has followed an equally straightforward solution to it. Hire more personnel to handle the larger volume of work. This solution is not unique to the court system, but is a common response to delay in bureaucratic agencies, Congress, and even the White House staff. In this broad context, the findings of this study—that delay in appellate courts is not totally dependent upon a heavy volume of work and is not remedied simply by increasing the number of personnel—are particularly important and surprising.

In examining what this means for government organizations generally, it is useful first to consider the extent and seriousness of delay described in the current study. Is it possible that the standard answers do not apply because there is not really a serious problem of delay in the courts studied?

The measures of delay presented by Martin and Prescott leave little doubt that by all available standards, including those of the American Bar Association (ABA) and of the appellate courts themselves, there is considerable delay in the appellate courts. In the four stages of appellate court activity looked at—the predecision phase; the perfection of the appeal to oral argument stage; the decision phase; and the post-decision phase—a large number of courts were consistently slower than either their internal standards or the ABA standards recommend.

How serious is this for the judicial process? Is it possible that speed is less a priority for appellate courts than for other branches of government? Does the work of appellate judges who are engaged in correcting errors made by lower courts and establishing precedents to guide future decisions demand more flexibility in timing than the decisions of politicians or bureaucrats? It is difficult to argue that this is the case—that delay by courts can be considered less of a problem than delay in other governmental organizations. It is easier to make the counter-argument, that the speedy resolution of court cases should always have had a high priority in the American system. Although delay in legislatures is considered by many people to be a necessary cost of democratic government, and slowness in the bureaucracy is regarded as both legendary and expected, there are different considerations involved in the court systems. The belief that "justice delayed is justice denied" is widespread. Courts make decisions that permanently alter the quality of individuals' lives. As the authors also have noted, appellate courts often determine whether a person will be compensated for injury or loss, freed from prison, or incarcerated for lengthy periods of time. Lives may be seriously disrupted as individuals await the final disposition of their cases, unable to make plans until the court has delivered its verdict. Society as a whole also has a strong interest in the timely settlement of disputes by the court system. Many people believe that crime and wrong-doing will not be deterred until its perpetrators are aware that courts will act swiftly to mete out punishment and that lengthy appeals and delays will not postpone the delivery of justice. Finally, taxpayers in their increasing demands for efficiency in government do not exempt courts from their scrutiny of how tax dollars are being spent. Speedy justice is generally considered to be of better quality and more effective than slow justice.

Since delay in appellate court systems exists and may be considered to be at least as serious a problem as delay in other parts of government, it is useful to examine the solutions proposed by Martin and Prescott and consider how they may also apply to other branches of government. The fundamental finding of the study seems to be that structural and organizational changes are necessary if excessive delay is to be eliminated in appellate courts. As has been previously mentioned, the common practice of simply adding more personnel to these courts has been questioned as a solution by the authors.

The solutions suggested include the following: shortening the amount of time allowed for filing cases; decreasing the number of extensions permitted per case; developing better methods of tracking cases accepted for appeal; scheduling oral argument automatically rather than waiting for it to be requested; eliminating circuit riding; adopting flexible case assignment procedures; adding a conflict-resolving mechanism to the court; instituting rules governing the amount of time allowed for submission of dissenting or concurring opinions; and developing standard clerical procedures for recording mandates. In general, these alterations in court structure and procedure strengthen the role of the appellate court judge, and in particular the chief justice, in controlling the flow of cases into and out of the court. As is noted in the study, if judges fail to exercise such expanded control, delay will probably not be reduced. Judges will become administrative bureaucrats under such reforms—responsible and accountable for the smooth and rapid processing of cases in their courts. Yet, Martin and Prescott have found that there seems to be no realistic alternative available if delay is to be reduced. This expanded administrative role of judges will itself have to be evaluated in light of its consequences for the court. It is possible that undesirable tradeoffs will be necessary if such a reformed system is to work. It may turn out that legal scholars with fine judicial temperaments will be excluded from appellate judgeships in the interest of getting better managers. Alternately, such a tradeoff may not occur. Good judges may make good managers.

Determining whether or not the solutions proposed by Martin and Prescott will work to reduce delay requires a period of experimentation and study. However, assessing the desirability of specific reforms seems to demand more than a simple determination of whether delay can be reduced by them. For, unlike increasing the number of court personnel to alleviate delay, many of the proposals put forth in this book, such as the increased administrative responsibility of judges, may alter the nature and functioning of appellate court systems in ways that extend beyond reduction of delay. The quality of justice delivered by the court may be affected. This is not to condemn such efforts to reform the courts, since, as has been pointed out, it is not unreasonable to assume that speeding up the work of the court in and of itself is likely to have a positive effect on the quality of justice produced. Timely court action is superior to slow action. But this immediate gain produced by speed must also be measured against broader standards of judicial behavior. As Martin and Prescott correctly point out, the most desirable standard against which to measure proposed reforms is one of high quality of justice. Since a recognized standard of this type does not presently exist, it may be useful to borrow standards that have been successfully applied to evaluating other types of governmental decisions.

Francis E. Rourke suggests that the quality of bureaucratic decision making should be measured against two standards: responsiveness and effectiveness.[1] Adapting these standards to the court, one would determine responsiveness by asking whether a proposed change in court structure or operations promotes a correspondence between the decisions of judges and the preferences of the community and members of the legal profession—lawyers, law professors, and judges. For example, does strengthening the control of appellate court judges over the delivery of materials from lower courts and the presentation of briefs by lawyers accord with accepted norms of how appellate

---

1. Francis E. Rourke, *Bureaucracy, Politics and Public Policy* (Boston: Little, Brown, 2nd ed., 1976), pp. 1-9.

courts should function? Is there any danger that members of the public entering the appellate system will feel "railroaded" by a more aggressive and inflexible time schedule for processing cases? The second standard, effectiveness, is "the degree to which [a system] leads to decisions that are more likely than alternative choices to bring about the outcomes that are desired."[2] This standard represents an effort to provide at least a crude indicator of whether or not reformed appellate systems would still produce the quality of justice expected of them.

If delay is reduced by introducing the new policies suggested by Martin and Prescott and the responsiveness and effectiveness of the appellate system are preserved, what are the implications of this for dealing with unwarranted delay in other parts of government? Or, to put this question another way, what does it mean if delay must be eliminated by reforming and reorganizing institutions rather than by increasing their resources? In the case of both Congress and the presidency, it means that the easiest solutions to slowness and delay are probably not going to work. Martin and Prescott's findings imply or suggest that, as many have suspected, for an organization like Congress to remedy problems of delay in its operations, it cannot simply increase the number of staff members. It must follow the advice of reform commissions like those headed by Richard Bolling and David Obey which have recommended far-reaching changes in establishing congressional rules and procedures. It suggests that presidents also will have to experiment with the structure of their executive office if they attempt to remedy problems of excessive delay in receiving advice from their staff.[3] Finally, in the case of the bureaucracy, these solutions, if verified, would indicate that despite well-documented problems with restructuring bureaucracies, this may be the sole practicable method of reducing delay within them.[4]

In summary, *Appellate Court Delay* raises significant questions about widely held beliefs concerning the causes of and solutions for delay in governmental decision making. If correct, its findings will have important consequences not only for reducing delay in appellate courts but also for attacking delay in other government institutions as well. The outcome of this type of rethinking—linking reform to structural changes rather than to increases in resources—has elements of irony. On the one hand it would seem to be another piece of supporting evidence for those who believe that "small is beautiful" and that big-spending, pro-growth liberals have been wasting the

---

2. Ibid., p. 3.
3. Stephen Hess, *Organizing the Presidency* (Washington: The Brookings Institution, 1976).
4. For a good look at the problems involved in federal reorganization, see Harold Seidman, *Politics, Position and Power: The Dynamics of Federal Organization* (New York: Oxford University Press, 2nd ed., 1976).

public's money. On the other hand, the suggestion that existing institutions may need to be restructured if their efficiency is to be improved and unreasonable delay within them is to be reduced should give pause to those interested in conserving institutions as they now exist. Martin and Prescott do not provide us with a conservative solution to the problem of delay in the appellate courts, but with a radical one, requiring careful but meaningful restructuring of the court system.

Delay in Appellate Courts
Comments on
Appellate Court Delay

Professor Robert A. Leflar
School of Law, University of Arkansas

It is almost an axiom in the law that justice delayed is justice denied. Much of what is troublesome by way of delay occurs while cases are docketed in the trial courts. Delay there can be attributable to pleadings, jurisdictional questions, lazy lawyers or judges, crowded dockets, unavailability of witnesses, and dozens of other causes.

Once final judgment is rendered in the trial court and appeal taken from that judgment, it would seem that there are few reasons for unnecessary delay. The case is stabilized in its record, and only appellate review (decision) is wanting. This of course does require some time. The pejorative term "delay" does not fairly apply to time that is useful in the normal operation of the appellate process; it fairly applies only to time that is wasted, used up unnecessarily or not used at all in the process. Before intelligent analysis can identify wasted time, it is necessary to know where in the process time is used up, how much, and (if possible) why.

There is a limit to the number of appealed cases that any seven-judge court, or any three-judge panel, can competently handle. It is generally agreed that no appellate judge, however competent, can write more than 35, or conceivably 40, full-scale publishable opinions in a year. The effort to write more risks shoddy opinions and the shirking of other duties, including the preparation of per curiam and memorandum opinions in less important cases. Less important cases are apt to be more frequent in intermediate than in top appellate courts, so that the average number of appealed cases per judge that can be properly disposed of by full-scale and lesser opinions will be somewhat larger in intermediate courts. When the total runs above 50 per judge in a supreme court, or above 75 or 80 per judge in a state three-judge intermediate panel, justice inevitably suffers. It becomes too hasty.

Persistently increasing numbers of cases filed in American state courts, with corresponding increases in the number of cases brought up to appellate courts, can give rise to unprocessed backlogs of appealed cases unless improved procedures, or at least changed ones, move the appealed cases along to decision more rapidly and efficiently. When backlogs develop, the backlogged cases are delayed.

One remedy often proposed is the creation of more courts—an

intermediate appellate court if none already exists, or more panels or districts if the state has already established an intermediate court. An alternative sometimes equally available, however, is the improvement of rules and procedures that can enable existing courts to handle the caseload more promptly. Admittedly, speedier procedures alone do not provide the whole answer. Speedy disposition of appeals can be a poor remedy; hurried justice may constitute justice denied just as surely as does justice delayed.

Backlogs, however, do not always justify more courts or more judges. The Kansas Supreme Court, deciding cases slowly and perhaps lazily, got badly behind in its docket late in the last century. The Kansas Court of Appeals, 1895 to 1901, cleaned up the accumulated cases, then was abolished, after which the Supreme Court, operating more efficiently, was able to take care of all the Kansas appeals for more than a half-century, until multiplying appeals justified the creation in 1977 of a new intermediate court. Joseph M. Hill was named Chief Justice of Arkansas in 1904, on a promise to clean up a big backlog, then resigned on February 1, 1909 with the docket up to date. Since then the Arkansas Supreme Court has decided its cases as promptly as any other American appellate court, and has been current with its docket at the beginning of each summer recess. The Supreme Judicial Court of Maine, operating as it had for a century with more regard for tradition than for efficiency, got badly behind in the early 1970s, but has now initiated improved procedures that enable it, at least for the time being, to handle all appeals promptly without establishing an intermediate court. Procedures for dealing with backlog and resultant delay, or with unwarranted delay regardless of backlog, at the appellate level are as diverse as the courts themselves.

It is possible to separate the two major causes of backlogs—increased volume and inefficient operation procedures—and to discuss one without tying in the other. That is sometimes done. Too many judges, disliking change and preferring to continue familiar ways of doing things, emphasize volume only and urge the creation of more courts so that they can decide the same number of cases in the same leisurely fashion as in days gone by, without worrying about an accumulating backlog. The other emphasis concentrates on how improved structural and procedural methods within existent courts can improve judicial performance, eliminate unnecessary delays, and handle increased volume without building up backlog.

The Martin-Prescott study, basically a statistical one, undertakes to identify the steps in the appellate process within which time lapses of varying lengths occur. The longest time lapses, and the most wasted time, are in the first step, between trial court judgment and the day when all appellate papers are filed so that the case is "at issue." The blame for this can be placed. It lies in the absence of responsible control of the appealing process by the appellate court, or by any other agency. The efficient and reasonably speedy completion of appeals has to be overseen by the appellate court; no other agency is able to oversee it. The lengths of time set for successive filings, the granting of extensions, and imposition of sanctions for unpermitted delays are all matters that, if vigorously administered by the court to which appeal is taken, could cut down substantially on these early delays.

Next in total lapse of time is the step between "at issue" and submission, either with or without oral argument. This is an area almost completely within an appellate court's own control. A good case management system is needed. Prompt scheduling of oral arguments; the use of central staff to identify issues and prepare preliminary memoranda; designation and prompt submission of cases in which oral argument is not needed; preargument settlement conferences, which can remove cases from the docket altogether; judicial reading of briefs and preparation of memoranda before cases are submitted— these and other techniques governed by the court can both shorten the time involved and improve the quality of justice achieved.

The steps between case submission and issuance of mandate normally involve shorter time periods, though the length of time between decision conference and approval of opinions is sometimes considerable. This can be controlled by court rules on circulation of draft opinions and on the time within which dissenting and concurring opinions must be prepared, plus the way in which decision and opinion conferences are conducted. There are courts in which the average time between submission and handing down opinions is less than a month, a result achieved by paying close attention to the court-controlled matters just mentioned.

The time between decision and mandate is presumably governed by a court's idea as to how long losing counsel should be allowed to file a motion for rehearing. This length of time ought to be no greater than the time allowed for filing notice of appeal from a trial court's judgment, and can fairly be shorter, though some courts, oddly, seem to allow more time.

The current study analyzes the times that elapsed, in the courts studied, as these times might have been affected by various procedures, parties, litigated issues, whether in civil or criminal cases, volume of appeals, backlogs, number of judges, conferencing methods, case assignment systems, professional staffs, sitting in divisions or panels as against en banc sittings, lengths of briefs, and other variables. The conclusion, essentially, is that none of these factors was shown, statistically, to have greatly affected the lengths of time inquired about. The only firm conclusion was that the time prior to "at issue" could be shortened if complete appellate supervision, instead of haphazard controls, were applied at all stages throughout that step.

The lack of relationship between the listed variables and the reported time lapses is not surprising. Once a court has established its standards, the time it takes to turn out its average cases, or any case of a given sort, is likely to be about the same, unless specific hurry-up procedures are employed. The study does show that heavy-volume courts had an average time lapse a little less than lower-volume courts, a result explained by the catch-up pressure in the busier courts.

Any procedure that can produce decisions in more cases within a given period of time operates to lessen delay just as surely as does one that shortens the time spent on each case. Good case management and other improved judicial procedures may not shorten the time any particular case is before the court, or even the average time. They can make a difference, however, in the number of cases the court can hear, so that an entire docket can be heard, dealt with more thoroughly, and even decided more speedily.

Court Delay and Queueing Theory

Comments on

Appellate Court Delay

Professor Alfred Blumstein
Urban Systems Institute, Carnegie-Melton University

The problem of delay due to congestion is a classic one, and has received a considerable amount of attention in the field of operations research. The body of theoretical models known as "queueing theory" has been developed to analyze the delay resulting from congestion and has been applied in the study of delay in systems as diverse as telephone networks, machine-shop tool rooms,[1] airport runways,[2] community correctional centers,[3] toll booths on bridges and tunnels,[4] as well as a wide variety of other service systems. Indeed, there have been a number of attempts to address delay in the courts by similar approaches, either through the simple formulas of queueing theory[5] or through more elaborate queueing simulations.[6]

Queueing theory models[7] consider "customers" arriving at a service facility, where there are one or more "servers" ready to serve them. If all the servers are already occupied with earlier arrivals, then the later arrivals must form a "queue" to await their turn to be served. Queueing theory is concerned with the statistical properties of the length of that queue and the associated delay experienced by

---

1. Georges Brigham, "On a Congestion Problem in an Aircraft Factory," *Operations Research*, Vol. 3, 412-28. (1955).
2. Alfred Blumstein, "An Analytical Investigation of Airport Capacity," unpublished Ph.D. dissertation, Cornell University (1960).
3. Carl M. Harris and T. R. Thiagarajan, "Queueing Models of Community Correctional Centers in the District of Columbia." *Management Science*, Vol. 22, 167-171. (October 1975).
4. Leslie C. Edie, "Traffic Delays at Toll Booths," *Operations Research*, Vol. 2, 107-138 (1954).
5. Norman Lyons, "Analytic Models of Criminal Court Operations," Ph.D. Dissertation, Carnegie-Mellon University (1972).
6. Joseph A. Navarro and Jean G. Taylor, "Data Analyses and Simulation of Court System in the District of Columbia for the Processing of Felony Defendants," *Task Force Report: Science and Technology*, Appendix I, 199-215 (1967) A Report to the President's Commission on Law Enforcement and Administration of Justice, U.S. Government Printing Office, Washington, D.C.
7. Harvey M. Wagner, *Principles of Operations Research* (Englewood Cliffs: Prentice-Hall, 1975), pp. 851 ff.

customers.[8] It is also concerned with the relationship between those measures of delay and the rate and pattern of arrivals and of the service process, as well as the organization of the service system, and the means by which arrivals are taken into service. In practice, these aspects of the service process might be modified in order to reduce the delay.

In many cases, such changes involve an economic or social cost. For example, the service rate can be increased by providing additional servers (an economic cost) or by diminishing the amount of service provided each customer (representing a potential social cost). In such cases, there is a tradeoff to be made between this cost involved in speeding the service and the benefits associated with the reduction in delay. The relationships derived, of course, can assist in making that tradeoff.

The simple formulas that have been developed in queueing theory are designed for the cases where the average rate and the average service rate are fixed, are constant over time, and do not vary as the length of the queue (or the "backlog") varies. A rich variety of theory has been developed to account for diverse statistical distributions of the arrival and of service-time patterns, to represent the many different processes by which customers are selected from the queue (e.g., simple first-come-first-served or multiple queues with different priorities assigned), to analyze networks of queues where completion of one service results in a customer's immediately entering a queue for a next step in the service process, and to account for many other variations on these themes.

One important aspect of queueing behavior in courts that seriously complicates any analysis of court delays, however, is the high adaptiveness of the "service rate" of a court in response to changes in the arrival rate of cases, or—more often because it is more easily observed—adaptiveness to the size of the queue or backlog. As the workload on a court varies, there is a rich repertoire of responses available to the court to modify its service rate to handle cases faster. In criminal trial courts, for example, as the input of cases (λ) increases, the backlog begins to grow, and that generates a pressure on the prosecutor, so that a greater proportion are settled by plea bargain (a very high service-rate mode), thereby raising the average service rate for the entire court to adapt to the increase in the arrival rate, thereby restoring the queue length or backlog to a more acceptable value. Thus, the fixed and observable service rate (μ), on which much of queueing theory is based, is replaced by an adaptive service rate,

---

8. In the simplest such case, if customers arrive at random at an average rate λ and spend an average time $1/\lambda$ being served (i.e., the service rate is μ), then an average arriving customer can expect to encounter a queue length $L = \lambda/(\mu - \lambda)$ and the delay associated with waiting in this queue is $W = \lambda^2/(\mu - \lambda)$. These results require that $\lambda < \mu$ (i.e., that arrivals do not come faster than they can be served).

which responds to the size of the backlog. Thus, the service-rate parameters of such a queueing system are "state dependent" (i.e., vary with the size of the queue). It is difficult to measure very well the nature of that dependency relationship, and so it is difficult to develop queueing theory models that characterize such queues.[9]

Indeed, one might postulate the adaptive behavior of courts to be such that the average service rate is continually adjusted to be equal to the average arrival rate, thereby keeping the size of the backlog fairly constant. If this is the case, queueing theory provides little help in estimating the size of the backlog, since decision making within the courts maintains a backlog whose acceptable value is generated by exogenous considerations. No queueing model adequately accommodates that kind of complex behavioral response, and formulations are needed that are much richer than those currently available. Thus, it might be appropriate to view court backlog as a manifestation of local legal "culture" and to estimate the factors in the local environment that are associated with backlog. This could be accomplished through a cross-sectional analysis of courts similar to that conducted by Martin and Prescott, but with size of the backlog as the variable of interest rather than court processing time. Relevant variables might include the number of lawyers in a jurisdiction and the number of cases per lawyer, in addition to the factors examined by Martin and Prescott. It has been shown in a wide variety of queueing situations, however, that $L = \lambda W$ (i.e., that the size of backlog is the product of the mean arrival rate and the average delay), and so the two studies might generate similar results. Since the arrival rates (λ) in different jurisdictions vary, however, a focus on backlog might well generate more sharply defined relationships than Martin and Prescott were able to discern.

Queueing theory models try to make a clear distinction between time spent in the queue (i.e., delay) and time spent being serviced (actual processing time). In the case of the court, those distinctions tend to become severely blurred. This results from the fact that multiple actors function as "servers" in the system. These include the judge or judges hearing a case, the attorneys on both sides (and their clerical or investigative staffs), as well as the variety of court functionaries such as court reporters. In any analysis of the sources and causes of court delay, it is important to distinguish between actual service time (T_s) and true delay time (T_d) spent waiting for a particular service. The sum of the two represents total processing time (T_p), i.e., $T_p = T_s + T_d$. Thus, for example, T_p is the time from filing of a case to the rendering of a decision, or, in the case of an appeals court,

---

9. Conway and Maxwell attempted to study queues with state-dependent parameters, but their model requires very restrictive behavioral assumptions. Richard W. Conway and William L. Maxwell, "A Queueing Model with State Dependent Service Rate," *Journal of Industrial Engineering,* 12:132-36 (1961).

from the rendering from the lower court decision until the final mandate by the appeals court; these T_p times represent the total time in the system, but not all of that time is attributable to delay—much of it is service time.

Although they often label it as "delay," it is this total processing time (T_p) that is the primary subject of attention in the volume by Martin and Prescott. Failure to maintain a clear distinction between total processing time (T_p) and true delay time (T_d) could lead to proposals to reduce "delay" (i.e., T_p) that fundamentally involve a reduction in T_s, leading possibly to a reduction in the quality of service that may be more deleterious than the benefits associated with faster processing. In general, reduction in the true delay (T_d) can be viewed as inherently good; a reduction in the actual service time (T_s) would also induce a reduction in T_d (through a reduction in congestion), and that, too, is good. But to the extent that the reduction in T_s represents a reduction in the *quality* of service, then that may be bad, and that cost must be weighed against the benefits in the reduction in T_d.

Thus, for example, T_p might well be reduced by reduction in the length of briefs or in the length of opinions (as was suggested by two of the correlations made in the Martin and Prescott study). Perhaps shortening these documents may make for even better "justice," and thus, *a fortiori*, they should be shortened. But shortening them may also diminish somewhat the quality of justice provided, at least in the jurisdictions where these documents are now long. And this could be true even when other jurisdictions manage *their* justice quite well— perhaps even better—with the shorter documents. When that is the case, then the change must be considered very carefully in terms of issues that go well beyond the reduction in processing time. The Martin and Prescott study suggests a number of approaches that might shorten processing time. Acting on those suggestions without first being sure that the correlation is truly causal, and then inquiring into the consequences of any such change on the quality of justice delivered, would be a violation both of the intent of their study and of responsible administration of the judicial process.

In examining processing time through the delay attributable to the courts, it is important also to distinguish delays resulting from queues in the court (where faster processing by the court would reduce the delay) from processing time as the case works its way to the court for the court's action. Thus, although a court might well chide one of the adversaries for delaying the other in bringing a case to the court, or might even intervene on the side of the delayed, this role in "traffic control" is very different from that associated with the actual processing done by the court. It might reasonably be argued that traffic control during the pre-filing period is not a court's role. However, the fact that roughly half of the total processing time from lower-court decision to appeals-court mandate is consumed there suggests that an appeals court that is pressed to speed up processing time might well direct its attention to this first step, at least as a defensive measure.

In directing its attention to this first pre-filing step, it is important for the court here also to distinguish among queueing delay associated with congestion, actual processing time associated with performing a task (e.g., generating a transcript), and "private procrastination delay" associated with each individual actor in the process.

Here, as in other aspects of the court process, a queueing theory approach—rather than the formulas of queueing theory—represents a useful framework within which to view the processing of cases through a court and the delays they experience in that process.

Other Publications of the Appellate Justice Improvement Project

PHASE I

Volume and Delay in Appellate Courts: Some Preliminary Findings From A National Study

Volume and Delay in State Appellate Courts: Problems and Responses

PHASE II

Volume and Delay in the New Jersey Superior Court, Appellate Division (March 1980)

Volume and Delay in the Montana Supreme Court (March 1980)

Volume and Delay in the Florida Court of Appeal, First District (April 1980)

Volume and Delay in the Colorado Court of Appeals (April 1980)

Volume and Delay in the Oregon Court of Appeals (April 1980)

Volume and Delay in the Illinois Appellate Court, First District (April 1980)

Volume and Delay in the Nebraska Supreme Court (April 1980)

Volume and Delay in the Ohio Court of Appeals, Eighth District (June 1980)

Volume and Delay in the Virginia Supreme Court (December 1980)

Volume and Delay in the Indiana Court of Appeals (December 1980)

The Appellate System in Oklahoma (Technical Assistance Report No. 1, January 1981)

The Appellate System in Kansas (Technical Assistance Report No. 2, January 1981)

The Appellate System in the North Carolina Court of Appeals (Technical Assistance Report No. 3, January 1981)

The Appellate System in New Hampshire (Technical Assistance Report No. 4, January 1981)

The Appellate System in Vermont (Technical Assistance Report No. 5, January 1981)

Case Tracking and Transcript Monitoring in Rhode Island: A Guide (Technical Assistance Report No. 6, January 1981)

Transcript Preparation in New Hampshire (Technical Assistance Report No. 7, January 1981)

A Survey of State Supreme Courts with Intermediate Appellate Courts (Technical Assistance Report No. 8, January 1981)

Appellate Justice Improvement Project: Collected Papers (January 1981)

The National Center for State Courts

The National Center for State Courts is a nonprofit organization dedicated to the modernization of court operations and the improvement of justice at the state and local level throughout the country. It functions as an extension of the state court systems, working for them at their direction and providing for them an effective voice in matters of national importance.

In carrying out its purpose, the National Center acts as a focal point for state judicial reform, serves as a catalyst for setting and implementing standards of fair and expeditious judicial administration, and finds and disseminates answers to the problems of state judicial systems. In sum, the National Center provides the means for reinvesting in all states the profits gained from judicial advances in any state.

Board of Directors

William S. Richardson, Chief Justice, Supreme Court of Hawaii, *President*
Theodore R. Newman, Jr., Chief Judge, District of Columbia Court of Appeals, *Vice-President*
Robert C. Broomfield, Presiding Judge, Supreme Court of Maricopa County, Arizona
Lawrence H. Cooke, Chief Judge, Court of Appeals of New York
Mercedes F. Deiz, Judge, Circuit Court of Oregon
Roland J. Faricy, Judge, Ramsey County Municipal Court, St. Paul, Minnesota
Joe R. Greenhill, Chief Justice, Supreme Court of Texas
Wilfred W. Nuernberger, Judge, Separate Juvenile Court of Lancaster County, Nebraska
Kaliste J. Saloom, Jr., Judge, City Court of Lafayette, Louisiana
Joseph R. Weisberger, Justice, Supreme Court of Rhode Island
Robert A. Wenke, Judge, Superior Court of California, Los Angeles County

National Center for State Courts Management Staff

Headquarters

Edward B. McConnell, Director
Keith L. Bumsted, Deputy Director for Administration
John M. Greacen, Deputy Director for Programs
Janice L. Hendryx, Acting Associate Director for Project Management
Lynn A. Jensen, Associate Director for Programs
Lynford E. Kautz, Associate Director for Development and Public Affairs
Joel S. Zimmerman, Associate Director for Research and Development

Regional Offices

Francis L. Bremson, Director, North Central, St. Paul, Minnesota
Samuel D. Conti, Director, Northeastern, North Andover, Massachusetts
James R. James, Director, Southern, Atlanta, Georgia
Lynn A. Jensen, Director, Mid-Atlantic, Williamsburg, Virginia
Larry L. Sipes, Director, Western, San Francisco, California